Python for Everyone

Mridula, Kamal Kumar Gola, Rohit
Kanauzia, Shikha Arya

Made with ❤ on the Notion Press Platform
www.notionpress.com

CONTENTS

PREFACE

Welcome to the world of programming with Python! Whether you're a complete beginner or an experienced coder looking to expand your skillset, "Python for Everyone" is here to guide you on your journey through the exciting realm of Python programming.

Python is renowned for its simplicity, readability, and versatility. It's a programming language that truly lives up to its name – it's for everyone. Whether you're interested in web development, data analysis, artificial intelligence, scientific computing, or simply automating everyday tasks, Python has something to offer.

In this book, we've crafted a comprehensive learning experience that caters to individuals at all levels. If you're new to programming, fear not. We'll start from the basics, gradually building your understanding of core concepts, syntax, and problem-solving techniques. For those with some coding experience, we'll dive deep into more advanced topics, exploring Python's powerful libraries and frameworks that can transform your ideas into reality.

Key Features of "Python for Everyone":

- **Progressive Learning:** We believe in a step-by-step approach that ensures you grasp each concept before moving on. From variables and data types to object-oriented programming and beyond, each chapter builds upon the previous one.
- **Real-world Examples:** Our aim is to bridge the gap between theory and practice. Throughout the book, you'll find practical examples and projects that reflect real-world scenarios, helping you apply your newfound knowledge effectively.
- **Hands-on Exercises:** Learning by doing is a fundamental principle of effective programming education. We've included hands-on exercises at the end of each chapter to reinforce your learning and provide opportunities for experimentation.

- **Comprehensive Coverage:** Python is a vast language with a rich ecosystem of tools. We cover a wide range of topics, including standard libraries, third-party packages, web development, data analysis, and more, so you can explore the areas that interest you most.
- **Tips and Best Practices:** Along the way, we'll share coding tips, best practices, and common pitfalls to help you write clean, efficient, and maintainable code.

Python's versatility means that once you've learned its fundamentals, the possibilities are endless. You might find yourself building websites, creating games, analyzing data, or even automating tasks to make your life easier. With "Python for Everyone" as your guide, you'll develop the skills and confidence to tackle any coding challenge that comes your way.

So, whether you're a student eager to embark on a programming journey, a professional seeking to enhance your skills, or simply someone who's curious about the world of coding, this book welcomes you. We're excited to have you join us on this adventure through Python, and we can't wait to see what you'll create.

Happy coding!

Mridula, Kamal Kumar Gola, Rohit Kanauzia, Shikha Arya

ACKNOWLEDGMENTS

Writing a book is a collaborative effort that involves the support, guidance, and encouragement of many individuals. We, the authors – Mridula, Kamal Kumar Gola, Rohit Kanauzia, and Shikha Arya – would like to express our heartfelt gratitude to all those who contributed to the creation of "Python for Everyone."

First and foremost, we extend our appreciation to our families – our kids and spouses – for their unwavering support and understanding throughout this journey. Your patience, encouragement, and understanding have been instrumental in allowing us the time and focus to bring this book to fruition.

We are deeply grateful to COER University for providing us with an environment that fosters learning and innovation. Our interactions with students and colleagues have been a constant source of inspiration, and we are thankful for the opportunities we've had to share our passion for programming.

A special note of gratitude goes to Prof. (Dr.) B M Singh, Pro Vice-Chancellor of COER University, for his guidance and support. Your belief in our abilities and your words of encouragement have motivated us to strive for excellence in this endeavor.

We would also like to extend our thanks to our colleagues, friends, and mentors who provided valuable insights, feedback, and suggestions throughout the writing process. Your expertise and constructive criticism have played a significant role in shaping the content and quality of this book.

Last but not least, we would like to express our gratitude to the readers of "Python for Everyone." Your interest in learning and your dedication to mastering Python programming motivate us to continue sharing our knowledge and experience.

In closing, we acknowledge that this book would not have been possible without the collective efforts of all those mentioned above, as well as many others who have supported us along the way. Thank you for being a part of this journey.

Sincerely,
Mridula
Kamal Kumar Gola
Rohit Kanauzia
Shikha Arya

INTRODUCTION

"Python is a language that is simple to learn, yet powerful enough to solve complex problems - Unknown"

Python is a high-level, interpreted programming language that was first released in 1991. It was designed to be easy to read and write, with a focus on simplicity and productivity. Python is open-source and can be used for a wide range of applications, from web development and data analysis to scientific computing and artificial intelligence. It has a large and active community of developers and users, who contribute to its development and support. Some of the key features of Python include its dynamic typing, garbage collection, and support for multiple programming paradigms, including object-oriented, functional, and procedural programming. Python also has an extensive standard library, which provides a range of pre-built modules and tools for developers to use.

Figure 1.1: Two snake logo of python

1.1 What is Python?

Python is a high-level, interpreted programming language that was first released in 1991 by Guido van Rossum. It was designed with a philosophy of simplicity and readability, with an emphasis on code clarity and ease of use. Python's syntax is simple and easy to learn, making it a popular language for beginners and experts alike.

Python is an open-source language, which means that it is free to use and distribute, and its code is publicly available for modification and improvement. This has helped to build a large community of developers who contribute to the language, creating libraries, frameworks, and tools that extend its functionality.

Python has many applications, including web development, scientific computing, data analysis, machine learning, artificial intelligence, and more. It has gained popularity in these fields due to its ease of use, flexibility, and ability to handle large amounts of data.

Python's popularity can be attributed to several factors. One is its simplicity, which makes it easy for beginners to learn and for experts to use. Another is its vast library of third-party modules, which allow developers to quickly and easily add functionality to their programs. Additionally, Python's popularity in the data science community has led to the development of many powerful libraries and tools for working with data.

Python has a wide range of frameworks and tools that make it an ideal choice for web development. These include Django, Flask, and Pyramid, which provide developers with powerful tools for building web applications quickly and easily. Python also has libraries for working with databases, such as SQLAlchemy, and for working with web services, such as requests and BeautifulSoup.

Python's popularity in scientific computing is due in part to its ability to handle large datasets and complex mathematical computations. Libraries such as NumPy, SciPy, and Pandas provide powerful tools for working with arrays, matrices, and data frames, while libraries such as Matplotlib and Seaborn provide visualization tools for creating plots and graphs.

Python is also widely used in machine learning and artificial intelligence. Libraries such as TensorFlow, Keras, and PyTorch provide powerful tools for building and training neural networks, while libraries such as scikit-learn provide machine learning algorithms for classification, regression, and clustering.

Python's simplicity, flexibility, and vast library of tools make it a popular choice for developers in many fields, from web development to scientific computing to machine learning and beyond. Its open-source nature and active community of developers ensure that it will continue to evolve and remain a powerful tool for many years to come. Table 1.1 shows the comparison between C, C++, Jav,a and Python.

Table 1.1: Comparison between Python, C, C++ and Java

Language	Type	Compiled/Interpreted	Application	Advantages	Disadvantages
Python	High-level	Interpreted	Scientific computing, data analysis, machine learning, web development	Simple syntax, rich libraries and frameworks, easy-to-learn	Slower execution speed, not suited for low-level programming
C	High-level	Compiled	Systems programming, embedded systems, device drivers	Fast and efficient, direct memory access, low-level hardware interaction	Steep learning curve, difficult to debug, not suited for rapid development
C++	High-level	Compiled	High-performance applications, game development, graphics, video editing	OOP features, fast and efficient, direct memory access	Steep learning curve, difficult to debug, not suited for rapid development
Java	High-level	Compiled/Interpreted	Enterprise software, web development, mobile development	Platform-independent, OOP features, safety and security features	Slower execution speed, requires a lot of memory, verbose syntax

Programmers often love Python because of its ability to increase productivity by eliminating the compilation step, resulting in a fast edit-test-debug cycle. Debugging Python programs is easy as it does not cause a segmentation fault. Instead, the interpreter raises an exception, and a stack trace is printed when the program does not catch the exception. Python's powerful introspection allows for source-level debugging, including inspecting local and global variables, setting breakpoints, and stepping through code. Adding print statements to the source code is also an effective debugging approach due to Python's fast edit-test-debug cycle.

It's worth noting that these are just generalizations, and the choice of language ultimately depends on the specific requirements of the application and the preferences of the developer.

1.2 Why python?

Python is a versatile and easy-to-learn language with a large and active community, making it an attractive option for beginners and experienced developers. It is also in high demand in fields such as data science and machine learning, with extensive libraries and frameworks that can be used for different tasks. Being open-source and freely available, Python is a popular choice for creating projects without worrying about licensing fees. There are several reasons why one should learn Python:

- **Versatility**: Python can be used for a wide variety of applications, including web development, data analysis, scientific computing, machine learning, and more. It has a large and growing ecosystem of libraries and tools that make it easy to work with many different types of data and technologies.

- **Ease of use**: Python has a simple and easy-to-learn syntax, which makes it a great language for beginners. It also has a large and active community of developers who contribute to its development and provide support through forums and other resources.

- **Career opportunities**: Python is widely used in industry, and there is a high demand for developers who have experience with the language. Learning Python can open up new job opportunities and help you advance your career in a variety of fields.

- **Open-source and free**: Python is an open-source language, which means that the source code is freely available and can be modified and redistributed by anyone. This makes it a great choice for hobbyists and developers who are just starting out, as well as for businesses and organizations that want to save money on software development.

- **Large community and ecosystem**: Python has a large and active community of developers and users who contribute to its development and support. This means that there are many resources available for learning and getting help with Python, including documentation, forums, blogs, and tutorials.

1.3   Installing Python

To install Python, follow these steps:

• Go to the official Python website at <u>https://www.python.org/downloads/</u>

• Download the appropriate version of Python for your operating system (Windows, Mac, or Linux).

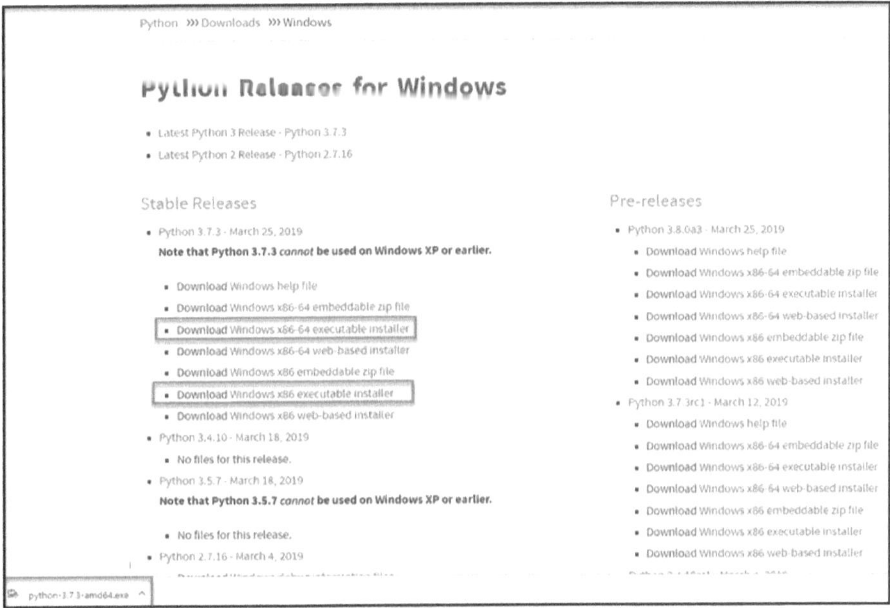

Figure 1.2: Example to download executable Installer for windows

• Run the installer file and follow the prompts to install Python on your system.

• If prompted, make sure to add Python to your system's PATH variable, which will allow you to run Python from the command line.

Once the installation is complete, open a command prompt (Windows) or terminal (Mac/Linux) and type "python" to start the Python interpreter. If Python is installed correctly, you should see a message that displays the version of Python that is installed on your system.

1.4.1   Setting up the development environment

To set up a development environment for Python, follow these steps:

- Install Python: First, make sure that Python is installed on your system (see previous answer for instructions).
- Choose an Integrated Development Environment (IDE): There are several popular IDEs available for Python, including PyCharm, Visual Studio Code, and Spyder. Choose an IDE that meets your needs and install it on your system.
- Install packages and libraries: Depending on what you plan to do with Python, you may need to install additional packages and libraries. These can be installed using pip, the Python package installer. For example, to install the NumPy library, you would type "pip install numpy" in the command prompt or terminal.
- Create a project: Once you have your IDE set up and any necessary packages installed, you can create a new Python project. This will typically involve creating a new file with a. py extension and writing your Python code in that file.
- Run your code: Finally, you can run your Python code using your IDE's built-in debugger or by running the code from the command line or terminal. To run a Python script from the command line, navigate to the directory where your script is located and type "python filename.py" (replace "filename" with the name of your file).

1.4.2   Running Python programs with example

To run a Python program, you first need to write the program and save it with a. py file extension. Here is an example Python program that prints the text "Hello, world!" to the console:

```python
print("Hello, world!")
```

To run this program, follow these steps:

- Open a text editor (such as Notepad, Sublime Text, or Visual Studio Code) and type the above code into a new file.
- Save the file with a. py extension (for example, "hello.py").
- Open a command prompt or terminal and navigate to the directory where the file is saved.

- Type "python filename.py" (replace "filename" with the name of your file) and press Enter.
- The program should run and print "Hello, world!" to the console.

Here is another example Python program that prompts the user for their name and then prints a personalized greeting:

```
name = input("What is your name? ")
print("Hello, " + name + "!")
```

To run this program, follow the same steps as above. When you run the program, it will prompt you to enter your name. Type your name and press Enter, and the program will print a personalized greeting to the console.

1.4.3 Using the Python interpreter

The Python interpreter is a tool that allows you to run Python code interactively, line by line. To use the Python interpreter, follow these steps:

- Open a command prompt or terminal and type "python" to start the Python interpreter.
- Once the interpreter starts, you can type Python code directly into the console and press Enter to execute it. For example, you can type "print('Hello, world!')" and press Enter, and the interpreter will print "Hello, world!" to the console.
- You can use the interpreter as a calculator by typing mathematical expressions directly into the console. For example, you can type "2 + 3" and press Enter, and the interpreter will print the result, which is 5.
- You can define variables and use them in your code. For example, you can type "x = 5" to define a variable named x with the value 5, and then type "print(x)" to print the value of x to the console.
- To exit the interpreter, type "exit()" or press Ctrl+Z followed by Enter.

Using the Python interpreter is a great way to experiment with Python code and learn the language interactively. It can also be useful for debugging code or testing small code snippets before incorporating them into a larger program.

Summary:
- Python is a high-level, interpreted programming language designed for simplicity and productivity.
- It was released in 1991 and is open-source, used for web development, data analysis, AI, and more.
- Python's features include dynamic typing, garbage collection, and support for various programming paradigms.
- It has a vast standard library with pre-built modules for developers to utilize.
- Python's syntax prioritizes readability and is easy for both beginners and experts.
- The language's versatility has led to its popularity in scientific computing, machine learning, and AI.
- Python fosters a large, active community of developers and users who contribute to its growth and support.
- The language is installed by downloading the appropriate version from the official Python website.
- Setting up a development environment involves choosing an IDE, installing packages with pip, and creating projects.
- Python programs can be run through the command line, with the Python interpreter, or in an integrated development environment (IDE).

Multiple Choice Questions (MCQ)
1. What is the primary focus of Python's design?
   a) Complexity
   b) Efficiency
   c) Simplicity and readability
   d) Speed
2. When was Python first released?
   a) 1995
   b) 2000
   c) 1985
   d) 1991
3. Which of the following programming paradigms does Python support?
   a) Procedural only
   b) Functional only
   c) Object-oriented only
   d) Object-oriented, functional, and procedural

4. Which term refers to Python's ability to run code without a separate compilation step?
   a) Interpretation
   b) Compilation
   c) Execution
   d) Iteration
5. What is the purpose of Python's standard library?
   a) It provides third-party packages.
   b) It offers basic programming functionality.
   c) It compiles Python code.
   d) It supports low-level programming.
6. What makes Python a popular choice for beginners?
   a) Complex syntax
   b) Difficulty in learning
   c) Simple syntax and readability
   d) High performance
7. Which programming field is NOT mentioned as a potential application of Python?
   a) Web development
   b) Data analysis
   c) Virtual reality development
   d) Artificial intelligence
8. Which library provides visualization tools for creating plots and graphs in Python?
   a) NumPy
   b) SciPy
   c) Matplotlib
   d) Pandas
9. Which library is commonly used for building and training neural networks in Python?
   a) TensorFlow
   b) SciKit-Learn
   c) NumPy
   d) BeautifulSoup

10. What is the significance of Python being open-source?
    a) It requires a license to use.
    b) Its code cannot be modified.
    c) It promotes a large community of developers and free distribution.
    d) It only supports certain programming paradigms.

Short Answer Type Question

1. Describe Python's primary philosophy in terms of code readability and simplicity.
2. What are some of the fields where Python is widely used? Provide two examples.
3. How does Python's open-source nature contribute to its popularity?
4. Explain the concept of an Integrated Development Environment (IDE) and give an example of a popular Python IDE.
5. What is the purpose of the Python interpreter, and how does it help in learning and development?
6. How can you install additional packages and libraries in Python, and what is the role of "pip"?
7. Briefly describe the steps involved in running a Python program from the command line.
8. How can Python be used as a calculator? Provide an example.
9. What is the significance of Python's extensive standard library?
10. Why might Python be considered a versatile language? Give two reasons.

Answer Key

MCQ

1. c) Simplicity and readability
2. d) 1991
3. d) Object-oriented, functional, and procedural
4. a) Interpretation
5. b) It offers basic programming functionality.
6. c) Simple syntax and readability
7. c) Virtual reality development
8. c) Matplotlib
9. a) TensorFlow
10. c) It promotes a large community of developers and free distribution.

VARIABLES AND DATA TYPE

"Python is the new BASIC." - John D. Cook

Python is a highly sought-after programming language in today's world, with developers prioritizing implementation over writing complicated programs. Python's ease of access and readability make it an ideal choice for this purpose. The fundamental concepts of any programming language are its building blocks, and this blog will focus on Python variables and data types.

2.1   What Are Variables?

Variables and data types in python as the name suggests are the values that vary. In a programming language, a variable is a memory location where you store a value. The value that you have stored may change in the future according to the specifications.

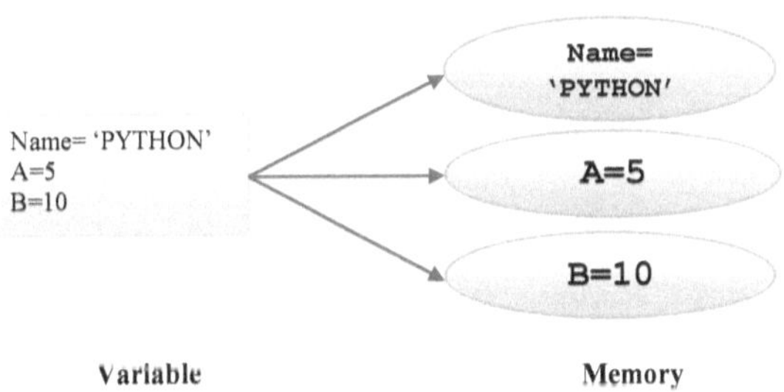

Figure 2.1: Variables in Python

In Python, variables are used to store values. A variable is a name that represents a value, and the value can be of different types, such as strings, numbers, or booleans. Here are some examples of variables in Python:

```python
x = 5 # integer
y = 3.14 # float
name = "John" # string
is_student = True # Boolean
```

In the above example, x is an integer variable with a value of 5, y is a float variable with a value of 3.14, name is a string variable with a value of "John", and is_student is a boolean variable with a value of True.

Python has several built-in data types, including:
- **Integers (int)**: Whole numbers, such as 0, 1, -1, 100, -100, etc.
- **Floating-point numbers (float)**: Numbers with a decimal point, such as 3.14, -2.5, 100.0, etc.
- **Strings (str)**: Sequences of characters, such as "hello", "world", "Python is awesome!", etc.
- **Booleans (bool)**: Values that represent True or False.
- **Lists**: Ordered collections of values, which can be of any data type.
- **Tuples**: Similar to lists, but they are immutable (cannot be changed after creation).
- **Dictionaries**: Key-value pairs, where each key is associated with a value.

Here are some examples of using these data types in Python:

```python
# integers
x = 5
y = -10
z = 0

# floating-point numbers
a = 3.14
b = -2.5
c = 1.0

# strings
name = "John"
message = "Hello, " + name + "!"

# booleans
is_raining = True
is_sunny = False

# lists
my_list = [1, 2, 3, "four", True]
```

```
# tuples
my_tuple = (1, 2, 3, "four", True)

# dictionaries
my_dict = {"name": "John", "age": 30, "is_student": True}
```

Understanding variables and data types is essential in programming because they form the building blocks of any program. By using variables and data types correctly, you can perform complex operations and solve real-world problems with Python.

2.2 Variables and Constants in python

In Python, variables are used to store values that can change during the program's execution. On the other hand, constants are used to store values that do not change during the program's execution. In Python, there is no built-in constant type, but you can use variables to store constant values by convention.

To define a constant in Python, you should use all capital letters to represent the variable name, and the value should not be changed throughout the program. Here's an example:

```
# define a constant
PI = 3.14159
# use the constant
radius = 5
circumference = 2 * PI * radius
print("The circumference of a circle with radius", radius, "is",
circumference)
```

In this example, PI is a constant that stores the value of pi, and it is used to calculate the circumference of a circle. By convention, we use all capital letters to represent PI to indicate that it is a constant.

On the other hand, variables are used to store values that can change during the program's execution. Here's an example:

```
# define a variable
x = 5
# use the variable
```

```
y = x + 3
print("The value of x is", x)
print("The value of y is", y)
```

In this example, x is a variable that stores the value of 5, and it is used to calculate the value of y, which is 8. Note that we can change the value of x later in the program if we want to.

Understanding variables and constants in Python is essential in programming because they help you manage values and perform operations on them. By using variables and constants correctly, you can write programs that are more readable, maintainable, and efficient.

2.3   Data Types in Python

Variables can store data of different types, and different types can do different things. In Python, a data type is a classification of values that determines the operations that can be performed on them. The data types in Python are as classified in Figure 2.2

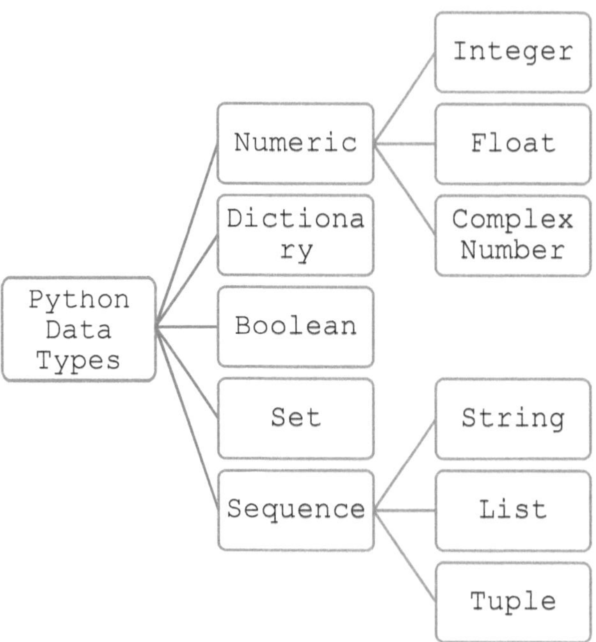

Figure 2.2: Data Types in Python

Python has the following built-in data types:

a. Numeric

b. Dictionary

c. Boolean

d. Set

e. Sequence

These data types with their examples are as described in the following section:

Numeric types: These are used to represent numbers. These are further classified as: integers, floating-point numbers (float), and complex numbers.

INTEGER	FLOATING POINT NUMBER	COMPLEX NUMBER
x = 5 z = 0	a = 2.5 b = -1.75	c = 2 + 3j d = -4j

Boolean: This data type has two values: True and False. It is used for logical operations.

```
is_raining = True
is_sunny = False
```

Sequence: A sequence is a collection of items that are in a deterministic order. The sequence in Python is in different forms as:

• **Strings**: These are used to represent text. Strings are enclosed in either single or double quotes.

```
name = 'John Doe'
address = "123 Main St."
```

• **Lists**: These are used to represent a collection of items that can be of different data types. Lists are enclosed in square brackets and separated by commas.

```
numbers = [1, 2, 3, 4, 5]
fruits = ['apple', 'banana', 'orange']
mixed = [1, 'apple', True]
```

- **Tuples**: These are similar to lists, but they are immutable (cannot be changed). Tuples are enclosed in parentheses and separated by commas.

```
numbers = (1, 2, 3, 4, 5)
person = ('John', 25, '123 Main St.')
```

Sets: These are used to represent a collection of unique items. Sets are enclosed in curly braces and separated by commas.

```
colors = {'red', 'green', 'blue'}
```

Dictionaries: These are used to represent a collection of key-value pairs. Dictionaries are enclosed in curly braces and separated by commas. Each key-value pair is separated by a colon.

```
person = {'name': 'John', 'age': 25, 'address': '123 Main St.'}
```

Understanding the different data types in Python is important because it allows you to choose the appropriate data type for your needs and perform operations on them. It also helps you to write code that is more efficient and easier to read and maintain.

In Python, the data type is set when you assign a value to a variable. Table 2.1 shows the initializing of all data types as discussed in section 2.3

Table 2.1: Examples showing the data type while assigning the value

Example	Data Type
x = "Hello World"	Str
x = 20	Int
x = 20.5	Float
x = 1j	Complex
x = ["apple", "banana", "cherry"]	List
x = ("apple", "banana", "cherry")	Tuple
x = range(6)	Range
x = {"name":"John", "age": 36}	Dict
x = {"apple", "banana", "cherry"}	Set

Summary

- Python is a highly popular programming language known for its simplicity and readability.
- Variables are memory locations used to store values, and Python supports various data types.
- Data types include integers, floating-point numbers, strings, booleans, lists, tuples, sets, and dictionaries.
- Variables can be used to represent different types of data, and constants store unchanging values.
- Numeric types include integers, floats, and complex numbers.
- Strings hold text data and are enclosed in quotes.
- Booleans have two values: True and False, used for logical operations.
- Lists are collections of items, while tuples are similar but immutable.
- Sets store unique items, and dictionaries hold key-value pairs.
- Data types help in efficient coding and choosing appropriate operations.

Multiple Choice Questions (MCQs)

1. What is the primary focus of Python's design?
   a) Efficiency
   b) Complexity
   c) Readability and simplicity
   d) Performance
2. Which of the following is NOT a built-in data type in Python?
   a) Integer
   b) String
   c) Character
   d) List
3. What is the purpose of variables in Python?
   a) To store constant values
   b) To store unchanging values
   c) To represent changing values
   d) To perform mathematical operations
4. Which data type is used to represent text in Python?
   a) Integer
   b) Float
   c) Boolean
   d) String

5. What are the two possible values of the Boolean data type in Python?
   a) 0 and 1
   b) True and False
   c) Yes and No
   d) On and Off
6. Which data type represents a collection of unique items in Python?
   a) Tuple
   b) Set
   c) List
   d) Dictionary
7. Which data type is used to store key-value pairs in Python?
   a) Set
   b) List
   c) Tuple
   d) Dictionary
8. Which data type is similar to a list but is immutable?
   a) Set
   b) Tuple
   c) Dictionary
   d) Float
9. Which data type is used to represent complex numbers?
   a) Float
   b) Integer
   c) Complex
   d) Numeric
10. What is the purpose of constants in programming?
   a) To store changing values
   b) To perform logical operations
   c) To store unchanging values
   d) To represent text data

Short Answer Type Questions:
1. What are variables, and why are they important in programming?
2. How can you define a constant in Python, and why do we use capital letters for constants?
3. Explain the concept of data types in Python.
4. Provide examples of three different numeric data types in Python.

5. How are strings represented in Python, and what operations can you perform on strings?
6. Briefly describe the Boolean data type and its two possible values.
7. Differentiate between lists and tuples in Python.
8. What is the purpose of a dictionary in Python, and how are key-value pairs stored?
9. How does a set differ from a list in terms of uniqueness of elements?
10. How does the concept of data types help in efficient coding and operations?

Answer Key:

MCQs:
1. c) Readability and simplicity
2. c) Character
3. c) To represent changing values
4. d) String
5. b) True and False
6. b) Set
7. d) Dictionary
8. b) Tuple
9. c) Complex
10. c) To store unchanging values

OPERATORS AND EXPRESSIONS IN PYTHON

"Python is the fastest growing language for data science." - DataCamp

Understanding operators and expressions in Python is important because it allows you to perform various operations on different data types and manipulate them according to your needs. It also helps you to write more efficient and concise code.

3.1 OPERATORS

In Python, operators are special symbols that perform specific operations on one or more operands. An operand is a value or variable on which an operator operates. Operators are classified as shown in figure 3.1

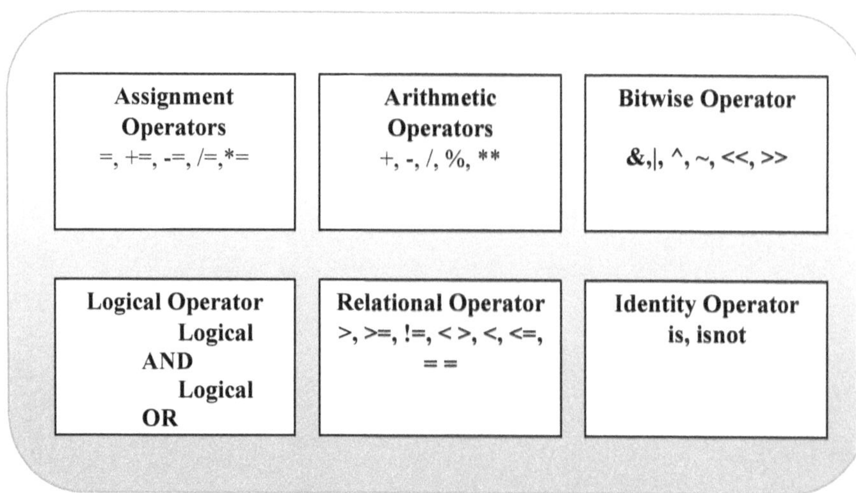

Figure 3.1: Classification of operators

3.1.1 Assignment Operators:

Assignment operators in Python are used to assign a value to a variable. There are several types of assignment operators in Python, which are listed in table below:

Operator	Description	Example
"="	This operator is used to assign a value to a variable.	x = 10
"+="	This operator is used to add the right operand to the operand and assign the result to the left operand.	x = 5 x += 3 print(x) Output: 8
"-="	This operator is used to subtract the right operand from the left operand and assign the result to the left operand.	x = 5 x -= 3 print(x) Output: 2
"*="	This operator is used to multiply the left operand by the right operand and assign the result to the left operand.	x = 5 x *= 3 print(x) Output: 15
"/="	This operator is used to divide the left operand by the right operand and assign the result to the left operand.	x = 15 x /= 3 print(x) Output: 5.0
"//="	This operator is used to divide the left operand by the right operand and assign the integer result to the left operand.	x = 15 x //= 3 print(x) Output: 5
"%="	This operator is used to get the modulus of the left operand divided by the right operand and assign the result to the left operand.	x = 15 x% = 4 print(x) Output: 3
"**="	This operator is used to raise the left operand to the power of the right operand and assign the result to the left operand.	x = 2 x **= 3 print(x) Output: 8

3.1.2 Arithmetic Operators:

Arithmetic operators in Python are used to perform arithmetic operations on numerical values. Below are the arithmetic operators in Python:

Operator	Description	Example
"+"	Addition operator that adds two operands together.	a = 5 b = 10 c = a + b print(c) Output: 15
"-"	Subtraction operator that subtracts the second operand from the first operand.	a = 5 b = 10 c = b - a print(c) Output: 5

Operator	Description	Example
"*"	Multiplication operator that multiplies two operands together.	a = 5 b = 10 c = a * b print(c) Output: 50
"/"	Division operator that divides the first operand by the second operand.	a = 10 b = 5 c = a / b print(c) Output: 2.0
"%"	Modulo operator that returns the remainder of the division of the first operand by the second operand.	a = 10 b = 3 c = a % b print(c) Output: 1
"**"	Exponentiation operator that raises the first operand to the power of the second operand.	a = 2 b = 3 c = a ** b print(c) Output: 8

"//"	Floor division operator that divides the first operand by the second operand and rounds down to the nearest whole number.	a = 10
		b = 3
		c = a // b
		print(c) Output: 3

3.1.3 Bitwise operators:

Bitwise operators in Python are used to perform bitwise operations on integer values at the bit level. Below are the bitwise operators in Python:

Operator	Description	Example
"&"	Bitwise AND operator that performs a logical AND operation between the bits of two operands.	a = 5 # 0101 b = 3 # 0011 c = a & b print(c) Output: 1 (0001 in binary)
"|"	Bitwise OR operator that performs a logical OR operation between the bits of two operands.	a = 5 # 0101 b = 3 # 0011 c = a | b print(c) Output: 7 (0111 in binary)
"^"	Bitwise XOR operator that performs a logical XOR operation between the bits of two operands.	a = 5 # 0101 b = 3 # 0011 c = a ^ b print(c) Output: 6 (0110 in binary)

Operator	Description	Example
"~"	Bitwise NOT operator that performs a logical NOT operation on the bits of the operand.	a = 5 # 0101 c = ~a print(c) Output: -6 (1010 in binary)
"<<"	Bitwise left shift operator that shifts the bits of the first operand to the left by the number of bits specified by the second operand.	a = 5 # 0101 c = a << 2 print(c) Output: 20 (10100 in binary)
">>"	Bitwise right shift operator that shifts the bits of the first operand to the right by the number of bits specified by the second operand.	a = 20 # 10100 c = a >> 2 print(c) Output: 5 (0101 in binary)

3.1.4 Logical operators:

The logical operators in Python use short-circuit evaluation. This means that if the result of the expression can be determined by the first operand, the second operand is not evaluated. For example, if the first operand of the "and" operator is False, the second operand is not evaluated because the expression can never be True. Similarly, if the first operand of the "or" operator is True, the second operand is not evaluated because the expression can never be False.

Operator	Description	Example
"and"	Logical AND operator that returns True if both operands are True.	a = True b = False c = a and b print(c) # Output: False
"or"	Logical OR operator that returns True if at least one of the operands is True.	a = True b = False c = a or b print(c) # Output: True
"not"	Logical NOT operator that returns the opposite Boolean value of the operand.	a = True c = not a print(c) # Output: False

3.1.5   Relational Operators:

Relational operators in Python are used to compare two values and return a Boolean value indicating the result of the comparison. Below are the relational operators in Python:

Operator	Description	Example
"=="	Equal to operator that returns True if the two operands are equal.	a = 5 b = 5 c = a == b print(c) Output: True
"!="	Not equal to operator that returns True if the two operands are not equal.	a = 5 b = 3 c = a! = b print(c) Output: True
"<"	Less than operator that returns True if the first operand is less than the second operand.	a = 3 b = 5 c = a < b print(c) Output: True
">"	Greater than operator that returns True if the first operand is greater than the second operand.	a = 5 b = 3 c = a > b print(c) Output: True
"<="	Less than or equal to operator that returns True if the first operand is less than or equal to the second operand.	a = 3 b = 3 c = a <= b print(c) Output: True
">="	Greater than or equal to operator that returns True if the first operand is greater than or equal to the second operand.	a = 5 b = 3 c = a >= b print(c) Output: True

3.1.6   Identity Operators:

Identity operators in Python are used to compare the memory locations of two objects. Below are the identity operators in Python:

Operator	Description	Example
"is"	Identity operator that returns True if the two operands are the same object.	a = [1, 2, 3] b = a c = a is b print(c) # Output: True
"is not"	Non-identity operator that returns True if the two operands are not the same object.	a = [1, 2, 3] b = [1, 2, 3] c = a is not b print(c) # Output: True

3.1.7 Membership Operators:

Membership operators are used to check the membership of an item in a sequence such as strings, lists or tuples. Python supports two types of membership operators as **in and not in**, shown as below

Operator	Description	Example
"in"	The operator returns TRUE if a variable is found in the specified sequence and FALSE otherwise.	num = [1, 2, 3, 4,5] a=4 c = a in num print(c) # Output: True
"not in"	The membership operator **not in** returns **True** if a variable is not found in the specified sequence and **false** otherwise.	num=[2,4,6,8] b= 5 c = b not in num print(c) # Output: True

3.1.8 Unary Operators:

A Unary operator works on a single operand. In python unary minus (-) operators negate the value of the operand i.e., the output is negative (if the operand is positive) or positive (if the operand is negative).

```
Example: b = 10
a = -(b)
print(a)
>>output: -10
```

3.2 Expressions

An expression is a combination of values, variables, operators, and function calls that evaluates to a value or produce results. We have many different types of expressions in Python. Expressions can be used in various contexts in Python, such as in assignments, function arguments, conditional statements, loops, and more.

Expressions can be simple or complex, and they can involve any of the operators and functions supported by Python.

<table>
<tr><td>

```
A literal expression
5
A variable expression
x
A function call expression
print("Hello, world!")
An arithmetic expression
2 + 3 * 4
A comparison expression
x > 5
```

</td><td>

```
A function call expression with
arguments
print("The sum of", x, "and",
y, "is", x + y)
An arithmetic expression with
parentheses
(2 + 3) * 4
A function call expression with
a method call expression
my_list.append(x)
```

</td></tr>
<tr><td align="center">

A Simple Expression

</td><td align="center">

A Complex Expression

</td></tr>
</table>

Since an expression is a combination of operators and operands that is interpreted to produce some other value, in any programming language, an expression is evaluated as per the precedence of its operators. So that if there is more than one operator in an expression, their precedence decides which operation will be performed first? To sort out these confusions, the operator precedence is defined. Operator Precedence simply defines the priority of operators that which operator is to be executed first. Operators with a higher precedence are evaluated first. Table 3.2 shows the order of operator precedence in Python, from highest to lowest:

Table 3.2: Operator precedence in Python

OPERATOR	PRECEDENCE
Parentheses: ()	HIGHEST
Exponentiation: **	
Unary plus and minus: +x, -x	
Multiplication, division, and remainder: *, /, //,%	
Addition and subtraction: +, -	
Bitwise shift operators: <<, >>	
Bitwise AND: &	
Bitwise XOR: ^	
Bitwise OR: |	
Comparison operators: <, <=, >, >=, ==,! =	
Logical NOT: not	
Logical AND: and	
Logical OR: or	
Conditional expression: if-else	LOWEST
Assignment: =, +=, -=, *=, /=, //=,% =, **=, &=, ^=, |=, <<=, >>=	

Summary

- Operators in Python are special symbols used to perform operations on operands.
- Assignment operators are used to assign values to variables.
- Arithmetic operators perform mathematical operations on numerical values.
- Bitwise operators operate on integer values at the bit level.
- Logical operators evaluate Boolean expressions and use short-circuit evaluation.
- Relational operators compare values and return Boolean results.
- Identity operators compare memory locations of objects.
- Expressions are combinations of values, variables, operators, and function calls that produce results.
- Operator precedence determines the order of evaluation in complex expressions.
- Understanding operators and expressions is crucial for performing operations and writing efficient code.

Multiple Choice Questions (MCQs)

1. What are operators in Python primarily used for?
    a) Storing values
    b) Displaying output
    c) Performing operations on operands
    d) Importing libraries

2. Which operators perform arithmetic operations on numerical values?
    a) Logical operators
    b) Bitwise operators
    c) Assignment operators
    d) Arithmetic operators

3. Which operator is used to assign a value to a variable?
    a) =
    b) +
    c) +=
    d) //

4. What does the modulus operator (%) return?
    a) Quotient of division
    b) Remainder of division
    c) Square root
    d) Exponentiation result

5. Which operator is used for bitwise NOT operation?
    a) ~
    b) &
    c) |
    d) ^

6. Which logical operator uses short-circuit evaluation?
    a) and
    b) or
    c) not
    d) xor

7. What do identity operators compare?
    a) Values of objects
    b) Memory locations of objects
    c) Data types of objects
    d) Bit patterns of objects

8. What does an expression in programming evaluate to?
    a) A variable
    b) A function
    c) A value or result
    d) A keyword
9. What is operator precedence?
    a) Order of evaluation in expressions
    b) Priority of variable names
    c) Order of function calls
    d) Order of assignment statements
10. Which operator has the highest precedence in Python?
    a) Comparison operators
    b) Bitwise operators
    c) Parentheses
    d) Exponentiation

Short Answer Type Questions
1. What are assignment operators, and how are they used in Python?
2. Explain the purpose of arithmetic operators in Python.
3. How are bitwise operators used, and what do they operate on?
4. Describe the short-circuit evaluation concept in logical operators.
5. What do relational operators in Python compare, and what values do they return?
6. What are identity operators, and how do they determine the equality of objects?
7. Define expressions in Python and provide an example.
8. What is operator precedence, and how does it impact the evaluation of expressions?
9. Differentiate between the "and" and "or" logical operators.
10. How do parentheses influence the evaluation of expressions?

Answer Key

MCQs

1. c) Performing operations on operands
2. d) Arithmetic operators
3. a) =
4. b) Remainder of division
5. a) ~
6. a) and
7. b) Memory locations of objects
8. c) A value or result
9. a) Order of evaluation in expressions
10. c) Parentheses

CONTROL FLOW IN PYTHON

CHAPTER
04

"Python is a great language for writing scripts to automate tasks and keep programs running." - Scott Hanselman"

In Python, control flow statements allow you to execute specific code based on certain conditions. Control flow in Python is the order in which the program's code executes. It is regulated by conditional statements, loops, and function calls. Figure 4.1 shows type of control flows statements in python

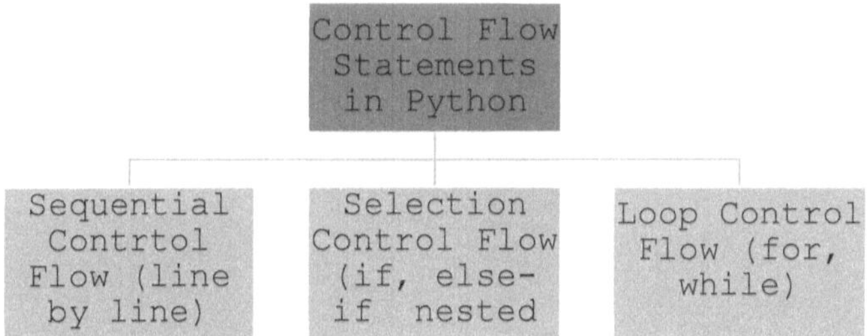

Figure 4.1: Types of control flow in Python

4.1 CONDITIONAL STATEMENTS

These statements allow you to execute specific code based on whether a condition is true or false. Some conditional statements are:

- if: This statement tests a condition and executes a block of code if the condition is true.
- elif: This statement is used to test multiple conditions. If the first condition is false, the elif statement will test the next condition, and so on.
- else: This statement is used to execute a block of code if all of the previous conditions are false.
- **Example**

  Code to print "Hello, world!" if the user's age is greater than or equal to 18:

- *age = int(input("What is your age? "))*
- *if age >= 18:*
- *print("Hello, world!")*

The basic conditional statement is the **if** statement, which looks like this:

```
if condition:
code to execute if condition is true
You can also include an else statement to execute code when the condition
is false:
if condition:
code to execute if condition is true
else:
code to execute if condition is false
```

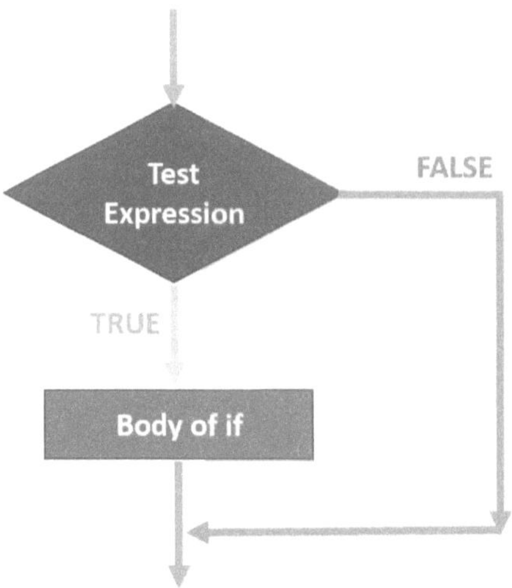

Figure 4.2: Flow Chart showing the 'if Statement' Execution

if-else in Python with example and explanation

In Python, the if-else statement is used to execute different code depending on whether a condition is true or false. The basic if-else syntax looks like this:

if condition:

    code to execute if condition is true

else:
     code to execute if condition is false

The condition is a Boolean expression that evaluates to either True or False. If the condition is true, the code inside the if block will be executed. If the condition is false, the code inside the else block will be executed.

Here's an example that uses an if-else statement to determine whether a number is even or odd:

```
num = 6
if num% 2 == 0:
print("The number is even.")
else:
print("The number is odd.")
```

In this example, the **condition** is **num% 2 == 0**, which is true if the remainder of **num** divided by **2** is **0** (i.e. if **num** is even). If the condition is true, the code inside the **if** block will be executed, which prints "The number is even." Otherwise, the code inside the **else** block will be executed, which prints "The number is odd."

if-elif-else Block

One can also use an **elif** statement to test multiple conditions. The **elif** statement is short for "else if," and it allows you to test additional conditions if the previous ones are false. You can use an elif statement to test multiple conditions:

```
if condition1:
code to execute if condition1 is true
elif condition2:
code to execute if condition2 is true
else:
code to execute if both conditions are false
```

Example that uses an **if-elif-else** statement to determine the grade for a student based on their test score:

```python
score = 75
if score >= 90:
grade = "A"
elif score >= 80:
grade = "B"
elif score >= 70:
grade = "C"
elif score >= 60:
grade = "D"
else:
grade = "F"
print ("The student's grade is:", grade)
```

In this example, the code checks each elif statement in turn until it finds one that is true. If none of the conditions are true, the code inside the else block will be executed. In this case, the student's score is 75, so the condition score >= 70 is true, and the grade is set to "C". The final line of code prints the grade.

Example that uses a while loop to print the numbers from 1 to 5:

```python
num = 1
while num<= 5:
print(num)
num += 1
```

In this example, the condition is num<= 5, which is true as long as num is less than or equal to 5. The code inside the loop will be executed five times, incrementing num by 1 each time. Once num is greater than 5, the condition will be false and the loop will end.

Both for and while loops can be useful in different situations, depending on the type of data you are working with and the task you are trying to accomplish.

Control flow statements are essential for writing complex programs in Python. By using these statements, you can make your code more flexible and adaptable to different situations.

4.2 LOOPS

Loops allow you to execute a block of code repeatedly. Some loops are:
- for: This loop repeats a block of code a certain number of times.
- while: This loop repeats a block of code until a condition is met.

There are two main types of loops in Python: **for** loops and **while** loops.

A **for** loop is used to iterate over a sequence of elements, such as a list or a string.

```
for variable in sequence:
block of code
```

Example

Code to print the numbers from 1 to 10:

```
for i in range(1, 11):
print(i)
```

A while loop is used to execute a block of code as long as a condition is true

```
while condition:
code to execute while condition is true
```

Example

Code to print the numbers from 1 to 10, but will stop if the user presses Enter:

```
number = 1
while True:
print(number)
number += 1
input()
```

The variable will be assigned each value in the sequence, and the block of code will be executed once for each value

4.4 RANGE FUNCTION

In Python, the **range** () function is used to generate a sequence of numbers. The basic syntax of the **range** () function is:

```
range (start, stop, step)
```

where start is the starting value of the sequence (default is 0), stop is the ending value of the sequence (not included in the sequence), and step is the step size between each number in the sequence (default is 1).

Here are a few examples to illustrate how the range () function works:

EXAMPLES

EXAMPLE 1

Generate a sequence of numbers from 0 to 9 (excluding 10) with a step size of 1.

for i in range (0, 10):

```
print(i)
Output:
0
1
2
3
4
5
6
7
8
9
```

EXAMPLE 2

Generate a sequence of even numbers from 2 to 10 (excluding 11) with a step size of 2.

for i in range (2, 11, 2):

```
print(i)
Output:
2
4
6
8
10
```

The **range()** function is commonly used in **for** loops to generate a sequence of numbers that can be used as the index of a loop. It is a powerful tool for generating large sequences of numbers quickly and efficiently in Python.

In Python, the pass statement is a placeholder statement that does nothing. It is used in situations where a statement is required syntactically, but no action is needed.

4.5 PASS STATEMENT

In Python, the pass statement is a placeholder statement that does nothing when executed. It is primarily used in situations where syntactically a statement is required, but no action is intended or necessary.

Lets understand one example.

```
for i in range(10):
Do something here
Pass
```

In the above code, the pass statement is used as a placeholder in the loop body where some code is expected. Since there is no actual code to execute, the pass statement is used to avoid a syntax error.

Another use of the pass statement is in function or class definitions when you want to leave the body of the function or class empty:

```
def my_function():
pass
classMyClass:
pass
```

In the above code, the pass statement is used in the body of the function and class definitions to indicate that no code is required at that point.

The pass statement is used as a placeholder in situations where a statement is required syntactically, but no action is needed. It is commonly used to fill in empty function or class bodies, or in situations where some code is expected but not yet defined.

4.6   Continue statement

In Python, the **continue** statement is used to skip the current iteration of a loop and move to the next iteration. It is commonly used in situations where you want to skip some specific elements in a loop.

Here's an example of how the **continue** statement can be used:

```python
for i in range(1, 11):
if i% 2 == 0:
continue
print(i)
```

In the above code, the **continue** statement is used to skip the current iteration of the loop if the value of **i** is even, and move to the next iteration. The **print()** statement is executed only if the value of **i** is odd.

The output of the above code is:

1
3
5
7
9

Another example of using the **continue** statement is in a while loop:

```python
i = 0
while i < 10:
i += 1
if i == 5:
continue
print(i)
```

In the above code, the **continue** statement is used to skip the iteration when **i** is equal to **5**, and move to the next iteration. The **print()** statement is executed for all values of **i** except for **5**.

The output of the above code is:

1
2
3
4
6
7
8
9
10

In summary, the **continue** statement is used to skip the current iteration of a loop and move to the next iteration. It is commonly used in situations where you want to skip some specific elements in a loop.

The break statement in python with example and explanation

In Python, the break statement is used to exit from a loop prematurely. It is commonly used in situations where you want to terminate a loop before it has completed all its iterations.

Here's an example of how the break statement can be used:

```python
for i in range(1, 11):
if i == 5:
break
print(i)
```

In the above code, the **break** statement is used to exit the loop prematurely when the value of **i** is equal to **5**. The loop terminates before completing all its iterations.

The output of the above code is:

1
2
3
4

Another example of using the **break** statement is in a while loop:

```
i = 0
while i < 10:
i += 1
if i == 5:
break
print(i)
```

In the above code, the break statement is used to exit the loop prematurely when i is equal to 5. The loop terminates before completing all its iterations.

The output of the above code is:

1
2
3
4

In summary, the break statement is used to exit a loop prematurely. It is commonly used in situations where you want to terminate a loop before it has completed all its iterations.

Summary
- Control flow in Python regulates the order in which code executes and is managed by conditional statements, loops, and function calls.
- Conditional statements (if, elif, else) allow executing code based on true or false conditions.
- Loops (for, while) enable repetitive execution of code blocks.
- Functions are reusable code blocks that perform specific tasks.
- The if-else statement is used to execute code based on true or false conditions.
- The elif statement tests multiple conditions if the preceding ones are false.
- The while loop repeats code while a condition is true.
- The for loop iterates over a sequence of elements, like lists or strings.
- The range () function generates sequences of numbers used in loops.
- The pass statement is a placeholder for situations where code isn't needed.
- The continue statement skips the current iteration in a loop, while break exits the loop prematurely.

Multiple Choice Questions (MCQs)

1. What does control flow regulate in Python?
   a) Memory allocation
   b) Code execution order
   c) Operator precedence
   d) Function definitions

2. What is the purpose of conditional statements in Python?
   a) Generate random numbers
   b) Execute code repeatedly
   c) Execute code based on conditions
   d) Perform mathematical calculations

3. Which statement is used to test multiple conditions in Python?
   a) while
   b) if
   c) elif
   d) else

4. Which type of loop is used to iterate over a sequence of elements?
   a) if loop
   b) while loop
   c) for loop
   d) elif loop

5. What are functions in Python?
   a) Random sequences
   b) Reusable code blocks
   c) Conditional statements
   d) Bitwise operators

6. What is the purpose of the range () function in loops?
   a) Generate random numbers
   b) Create lists
   c) Define conditions
   d) Generate sequences of numbers

7. What is the use of the pass statement?
   a) Define function arguments
   b) Exit a loop prematurely
   c) Skip an iteration in a loop
   d) Act as a placeholder

8. What does the continue statement do in a loop?
   a) Exits the loop prematurely
   b) Skips the current iteration
   c) Terminates the program
   d) Breaks the loop completely
9. Which statement is used to exit a loop prematurely in Python?
   a) pass
   b) continue
   c) return
   d) break
10. How can the if-else statement be used to execute different code paths?
    a) By providing multiple conditions separated by commas
    b) By using only, the if statement
    c) By testing the same condition repeatedly
    d) By using the elif statement

Short Answer Type Questions:
1. What are conditional statements, and how do they control the execution of code?
2. Explain the purpose of for and while loops in Python.
3. What is the difference between the if-else statement and the elif statement?
4. How is the pass statement used in Python, and in what situations?
5. Describe how the range () function is used in a for loop.
6. When and why would you use the continue statement in a loop?
7. What does the break statement do, and how does it affect loops?
8. How does the if-elif-else statement sequence work in determining the output?
9. Explain the concept of short-circuit evaluation in Python's logical operators.
10. How can functions in Python aid in code reusability and organization?

Answer Key

MCQs

1. b) Code execution order
2. c) Execute code based on conditions
3. c) elif
4. c) for loop
5. b) Reusable code blocks
6. d) Generate sequences of numbers
7. d) Act as a placeholder
8. b) Skips the current iteration
9. d) break
10. d) By using the elif statement

FUNCTIONS IN PYTHON

"Python is powerful… and fast; plays well with others; runs everywhere; is friendly and easy to learn; is open." - Python.org

5.1 Introduction

In Python programming, functions play a crucial role in organizing and reusing code. They are essential tools for breaking down complex problems into manageable pieces and promoting code modularity. By encapsulating a set of instructions within a named block, functions allow us to execute specific tasks repeatedly without duplicating code. Understanding how to define, call, and use functions effectively is fundamental to becoming proficient in Python.

This chapter provides a comprehensive overview of functions in Python, covering their syntax, parameters, return values, and various aspects of function usage. We will explore the process of defining functions, examining the importance of function signatures, and discussing best practices for choosing descriptive and meaningful names. Moreover, we will delve into the different ways of calling functions, including positional and keyword arguments, to provide flexibility and clarity in function invocations.

Furthermore, the chapter explores built-in functions, such as mathematical and string functions, which are readily available in Python's standard library. These built-in functions offer a wide range of functionality, enabling developers to perform common operations efficiently.

Additionally, we will touch on the concept of recursion—a powerful technique where a function calls itself—which can be used to solve complex problems by breaking them down into smaller, self-referential subproblems.

By the end of this chapter, you will have a solid understanding of functions in Python and be equipped with the knowledge to leverage their power and flexibility in your own programming endeavors.

5.2 Defining Functions

Functions in Python allow you to encapsulate a set of instructions into a named block, which can be executed repeatedly throughout your code. Defining a function involves specifying its name, parameters (optional), and the block of code it contains.

The basic notation of function categorized it into two types as:

- **Built-In functions:** These are pre-defined functions that are available in Python without the need for any additional import statements. Examples include print (), len(), type(), and range().

- **User-Defined function:** These functions are created by the user to perform specific tasks. They are defined using the *def* keyword followed by a function name, parameters (if any), and a block of code. User-defined functions allow code reuse and modular programming.

Syntax

The syntax for defining a function in Python is straightforward. It begins with the keyword def, followed by the function name and a pair of parentheses. If the function requires parameters, they are specified within the parentheses. The function definition is then followed by a colon (:) to indicate the start of the function body. The body of the function is indented under the def statement to distinguish it from the rest of the code.

def function_name(parameters): *# Function body*
 # Code to be executed

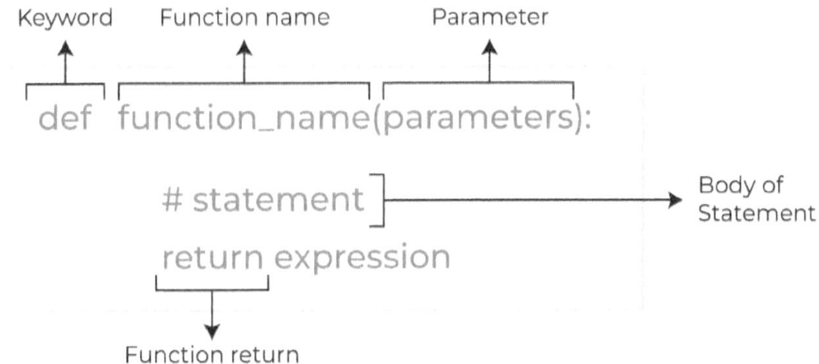

Figure 5.1: Function definition

5.2.1 Parameters

Functions can accept parameters, which are variables that allow you to pass values into the function. Parameters are specified within the parentheses after the function name. You can define multiple parameters by separating them with commas. These parameters act as placeholders that will take on the values passed to the function when it is called.

5.2.2 Return Values

A function can optionally return a value after performing its operations. The return statement is used to specify the value to be returned. This allows the function to pass computed results or information back to the code that called it. The return statement also terminates the execution of the function.

```
def add_numbers(a, b): sum = a + b
return sum
```

In the above example, the add numbers function takes two parameters (a and b) and returns their sum. The return statement sends the computed sum back to the caller.

5.3 Types of Functions

In Python, there are some other types of functions that serve different purposes. Here are some commonly used types of functions in Python:

1. **Lambda Functions** (Anonymous Functions): These are small, one-line functions that do not have a name. They are created using the lambda keyword and are often used for simple tasks or as arguments to higher-order functions.

2. **Recursive Functions**: A recursive function is a function that calls itself during its execution. It is used to solve problems that can be divided into smaller subproblems. Recursive functions must have a base case to terminate the recursion.

3. **Higher-Order Functions**: These functions take one or more functions as arguments or return a function as a result. Examples of higher-order functions include map(), filter(), and reduce().

4. **Generator Functions**: These functions use the yield keyword instead of return to return a sequence of values. Generator functions produce a series of values one at a time and are memory-efficient compared to returning a complete list.

5. **Decorator Functions**: Decorators are functions that modify the behavior of other functions without changing their source code. They are defined using the @ symbol followed by the decorator name above the function definition.

6. **Method Functions**: These functions are defined inside classes and are associated with specific instances or the class itself. They are called using the dot notation and have access to the instance or class attributes.

5.4   Function Call

Once you have defined a function in Python, you can call it to execute the code within the function body. Calling a function involves using the function name followed by a pair of parentheses. If the function requires arguments, you provide them within the parentheses and call a function using the function name followed by parentheses:

```
function_name(argument1,argument2, …)
```

```
# You can also define your own functions using the def keyword:
def function_name (parameter1, parametert2, …):
code to execute when the function is called
return value optional
#function calling by passing the actual values in function parameters
function_name (argument1, argument2, …)
```

Parameters vs Arguments:

Parameters are used as variables to define the functions inside the parentheses () followed by function_name. Whereas the arguments are the actual parameters, used at the time of function call. Arguments are the values or actual values that are passed to the function parameters for performing the specific task.

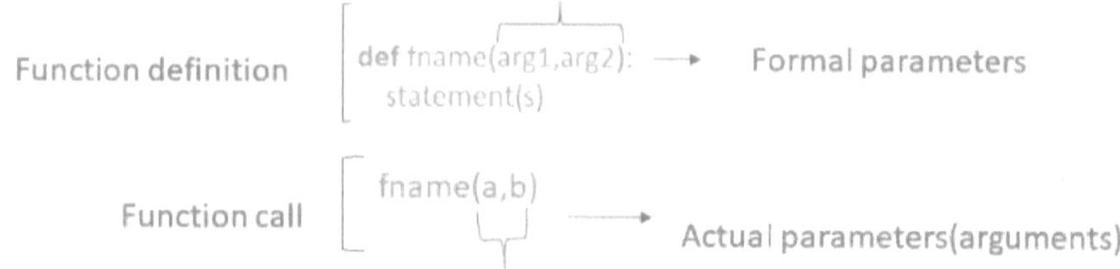

On the basis of arguments type in Python, we have the following Python function arguments:

5.4.1 Positional Arguments

The most common way to call a function is by providing positional arguments. Positional arguments are passed to the function in the order specified in the function definition. For example, if a function expects two parameters, you need to provide values for those parameters in the same order.

```
def greet (name, message): print("Hello,", name + "!") print(message)
greet ("Alice", "How are you today?")
```

In the above example, the function greet takes two parameters: name and message. When calling the function, we pass the arguments "Alice" and "How are you today?" in the same order as the parameters.

5.4.2 Keyword Arguments

Python also supports keyword arguments, where you explicitly specify the parameter name followed by its corresponding value when calling a function. This allows you to provide arguments in any order, making your function calls more flexible and self-explanatory.

```
def calculate_total(price, quantity): total = price * quantity
print("Total cost:", total)
calculate_total(price=10, quantity=5)
```

In the above example, the calculate_total function takes two parameters: price and quantity. By using keyword arguments, we can explicitly assign values to these parameters when calling the function. This approach is particularly useful when dealing with functions that have many parameters or when you want to provide clarity and self-documentation to your function calls.

Using keyword arguments can also be combined with positional arguments, giving you more flexibility in function calls.

calculate_total(10, quantity=5)

In this case, we provide a positional argument for price and a keyword argument for quantity.

5.4.3 Default Arguments:

In default arguments, we can set the default value to the arguments which are used for any missing arguments.

```
def greet (name, message= 'Hello'):
print (f '{message}, {name}!')
greet ('Allen')
greet ('John', 'Hey')
```

Here is the output of the first call to greet function print **Hello, Allen!** Which takes the message as a default argument.

Note: Non-default arguments cannot be followed by default arguments. i.e. we have default values for all the arguments to their right

5.4.4 Arbitrary Arguments:

This type of argument is used when the number of arguments is not known by the programmer. Arbitrary arguments are versatile for the code. Arbitrary arguments are represented by an asterisk (*) before the parameter in the function and its also known as ***args** in Python, here **args** is just a notation. We can use any other argument name instead of it.

```
def class_student(*name):
print('registered Student list ')
for i in name:
print(i)
class_student('Ash', 'Riya', 'James', 'Jojo')
```

By utilizing different types of arguments effectively, you can call functions with the appropriate values and ensure the desired behavior of your code.

5.5 Built-in Functions

Python provides a rich set of built-in functions that are readily available in its standard library. These functions offer a wide range of functionality, allowing you to perform common operations efficiently without having to implement them from scratch. In this section, we will explore some commonly used categories of built-in functions.

5.5.1 Math Functions

Python's standard library includes various math functions that enable you to perform mathematical computations. These functions cover a wide range of operations, including basic arithmetic, trigonometry, logarithms, rounding, and more. Some commonly used math functions include:

- abs(): Returns the absolute value of a number.
- round(): Rounds a number to the nearest integer or a specified number of decimal places.
- max(): Returns the maximum value from a sequence of values.
- min(): Returns the minimum value from a sequence of values.
- pow(): Raises a number to a specified power.
- sqrt(): Calculates the square root of a number.

These math functions can be particularly useful when performing complex mathematical calculations or manipulating numerical data.

5.5.2 String Functions

Working with strings is a fundamental aspect of programming, and Python provides a range of built-in string functions to facilitate string manipulation and analysis. These functions allow you to perform tasks such as concatenation, searching, case conversion, substring extraction, and more. Some commonly used string functions include:

- len(): Returns the length of a string.
- upper(): Converts a string to uppercase.
- lower(): Converts a string to lowercase.
- split(): Splits a string into a list of substrings based on a delimiter.
- join(): Joins a list of strings into a single string using a specified delim- iter.
- find(): Searches for a substring within a string and returns its index.

These string functions provide powerful tools for manipulating and analyzing text data in Python.

By utilizing these built-in functions, you can leverage the functionality pro- vided by Python's standard library and save time and effort in your coding endeavors.

5.6 Recursion

Recursion is a powerful concept in programming where a function calls itself to solve a problem by breaking it down into smaller, self-referential subproblems. It is based on the principle of divide and conquer, where a complex problem is divided into simpler and more manageable subproblems until a base case is reached. Recursion provides an elegant and efficient way to solve certain types of problems that exhibit recursive patterns.

5.6.1 Recursive Functions

A recursive function is a function that calls itself within its own body. This self-referential call allows the function to break down the problem into smaller instances of the same problem until it reaches a base case. The base case is the condition that determines when the recursion should stop and provides the final result.

```
def factorial(n):
if n == 0:
return 1
else:
return n * factorial(n-1)
```

In the above example, the factorial function calculates the factorial of a number n. It calls itself with a smaller value n-1 until it reaches the base case when n is 0. The function then returns 1, which acts as the terminating condition for the recursion. The results of the recursive calls are then multiplied together to obtain the final factorial value.

5.6.2 Base Case

The base case is a critical aspect of recursion as it prevents infinite recursion and provides the stopping condition for the function. Without a base case, the recursive function would continue calling itself indefinitely, leading to a stack overflow error.

A well-designed recursive function defines one or more base cases that directly handle the simplest possible instance of the problem. Once the base case is reached, the function returns a specific value or performs a specific action to end the recursion.

When designing recursive algorithms, it is crucial to identify the base case(s) that will terminate the recursion and ensure that the problem is broken down into smaller subproblems with each recursive call.

Recursion can be a powerful tool for solving problems that can be naturally divided into smaller, similar subproblems. However, it is important to use recursion judiciously and ensure that the problem lends itself well to a recursive approach, as it can be less efficient in certain situations.

By understanding the principles and techniques of recursion, you can solve complex problems effectively and elegantly in your Python programs.

5.7 Conclusion

In this chapter, we have explored the concept of functions in Python and their importance in organizing and reusing code. Functions allow us to encapsulate a set of instructions into a named block, promoting code modularity and facilitating code maintenance. By defining functions, we can break down complex problems into manageable pieces and improve the overall structure and readability of our programs.

We discussed the process of defining functions, including their syntax and the use of parameters and return values. Defining functions with meaningful names and clear function signatures is crucial for writing maintainable and understandable code.

Furthermore, we covered the various ways to call functions, including positional and keyword arguments. Understanding how to pass values to functions correctly enhances the flexibility and readability of your code.

Additionally, we explored the power of built-in functions, which offer a wide range of functionality for performing common operations efficiently. Python's standard library provides a rich set of math functions and string functions that enable you to manipulate data effectively.

Finally, we delved into the concept of recursion, a powerful technique for solving problems by breaking them down into smaller, self-referential sub problems. Recursion allows for elegant and concise code solutions, particularly for problems that exhibit recursive patterns.

By mastering the concepts and techniques presented in this chapter, you are now equipped with the knowledge and tools to utilize functions effectively in your Python programs. Functions provide a foundation for code organization, reusability, and problem-solving. As you continue your programming journey, make sure to apply these concepts in your projects and explore more advanced topics related to functions in Python.

Summary:

- Functions in Python are essential for organizing and reusing code.
- They encapsulate a set of instructions within a named block, promoting code modularity.
- Functions help break down complex problems into manageable pieces.
- Defining functions involves specifying a name, parameters, and a code block.
- Parameters act as placeholders for values passed to the function.
- Functions can return values using the **return** statement.
- Python has various types of functions: built-in, user-defined, lambda, recursive, etc.
- Recursive functions call themselves to solve problems by breaking them down.
- Base case is crucial in recursion to prevent infinite loops.
- Built-in functions cover math and string operations, among others.
- Functions can be called with positional or keyword arguments.
- Proper usage of functions improves code readability and reusability.

MCQs

1. What is the primary purpose of functions in Python?
   A) Aesthetic code formatting
   B) Simplifying code compilation
   C) Reusing and organizing code
   D) Enhancing runtime speed
2. Which keyword is used to define a function in Python?
   A) function
   B) define
   C) func
   D) def
3. What is a base case in recursive functions?

    A) The initial value of a variable

    B) A case that requires further recursion

    C) A condition that terminates the recursion

    D) The largest value in a recursive sequence

4. Which function is used to find the length of a string in Python?

    A) len()

    B) length()

    C) count()

    D) size()

5. Which type of argument allows you to specify the parameter name when calling a function?

    A) Ordinal arguments

    B) Indexed arguments

    C) Positional arguments

    D) Keyword arguments

Short Answer Questions

1. What is the purpose of the **return** statement in a function?
2. Explain the concept of recursion in programming.
3. How can keyword arguments improve the clarity of function calls?
4. Describe the role of the base case in recursive functions.
5. Give an example of a built-in function for string manipulation.
6. What is the significance of using meaningful names for functions?
7. How does Python's standard library help in coding efficiency?
8. What are lambda functions, and when are they commonly used?
9. How can functions enhance code modularity?
10. What are positional arguments, and how are they passed to a function?

Answer Key

MCQs

1. C Reusing and organizing code
2. D def
3. C A condition that terminates the recursion
4. A len()
5. D Keyword arguments

MODULES

"Python is an experiment in how much freedom programmers need. Too much freedom and nobody can read another's code; too little and expressiveness is endangered." - Guido van Rossum

Introduction

In Python programming, modules play a vital role in organizing, reusing, and extending code. Modules are collections of Python code grouped together to form a cohesive unit, offering a way to organize related functions, classes, and variables. They provide a means to break down complex systems into manageable components and promote code reusability across projects.

This chapter provides a comprehensive exploration of modules in Python, covering their definition, benefits, and usage. We will delve into the process of importing modules, enabling us to access their contents and leverage their functionality within our code. Whether it's using modules from the Python standard library or creating custom modules, this chapter will guide you through the various techniques and best practices.

The chapter also focuses on commonly used standard library modules, which provide a vast array of ready-to-use functionality for tasks such as mathematical computations, date and time operations, file handling, and more. Understanding how to leverage these modules will significantly enhance your productivity as a Python programmer.

Additionally, you will learn how to create your own custom modules, encapsulating related code an,d creating reusable components. We will explore techniques for organizing and structuring modules, including proper naming conventions, documentation practices, and scoping.

By the end of this chapter, you will have a solid understanding of modules in Python and how to effectively use both standard library modules and custom modules. This knowledge will empower you to write modular, reusable, and maintainable code, saving time and effort in your Python projects.

Let's begin our journey into the world of modules in Python!

6.1 What are Modules?

Modules in Python are self-contained units of code that allow you to organize related functionality into separate files. A module is essentially a Python script that can be imported and used by other Python programs. It provides a way to break down a complex program into smaller, more manageable parts, promoting code reuse and modularity.

6.1.1 Definition

In simple terms, a module is a file containing Python definitions, statements, and functions. It can include variables, classes, and other components that can be accessed and utilized by other Python programs. Modules typically have a '.py' extension and can be created by simply saving a Python script with the desired functionality.

Types of Modules
- **Built-in Modules**: Python comes with a rich set of built-in modules that provide a wide range of functionality. These modules are part of the Python standard library and can be used directly without the need for additional installation. Examples include math, random, datetime, os, and sys.
- **Third-Party Modules**: These are modules developed by individuals or organizations outside of the Python standard library. They provide additional functionality not available in the built-in modules. Third-party modules can be installed using package managers like pip. Popular third-party modules include numpy, pandas, matplotlib, and requests.
- **Custom Modules**: These are user-defined modules created by Python programmers to encapsulate reusable code. A custom module is simply a Python script containing functions, classes, or variables that can be imported and used in other programs. Custom modules are useful for organizing code and promoting code reusability.
- **Package Modules**: A package is a way of organizing related modules into a directory hierarchy. It consists of a directory that contains a special file called __init__.py. Packages allow you to group related modules together and provide a namespace for the modules within the package. They facilitate modular and structured programming.

- **Namespace Packages**: Unlike regular packages, namespace packages do not require an __init__.py file. They are used to create a package-like structure without the need for a common directory hierarchy. Namespace packages are often used when multiple organizations or projects want to contribute to a shared package or library.

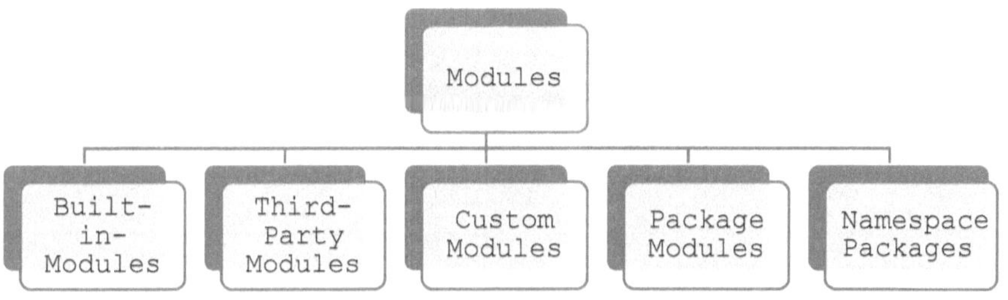

Figure 6.1 Types of Modules

6.1.2 Benefits of Using Modules

Using modules in your Python programs offers several benefits:

- Code Organization and Reusability: Modules provide a logical way to organize related code into separate units, making it easier to navigate and maintain large projects. By encapsulating re- lated functionality, modules promote code reusability across different programs, reducing code duplication and improving overall development efficiency.

- Modularity: Modular programming is a software design technique that emphasizes building programs from small, independent modules. By using modules in Python, you can break down complex systems into smaller, more manageable components, each responsible for a specific functionality. This modular approach enhances code readability, maintainability, and flexibility.

- Namespace Isolation: Modules provide a separate namespace for the code they contain. This means that the names of variables, functions, and classes defined within a module do not clash with names defined in other modules or the main program. Names- pace isolation helps avoid naming conflicts and provides a clean and organized structure to your code.

6.1.3 Module Importing

To use a module in Python, you need to import it into your program. Importing a module makes its functionality available for use within your code. Python provides various ways to import modules:

Importing Entire Modules

The simplest way to import a module is to use the 'import' statement followed by the module name:

```
import module_name
```

This allows you to access the functions, variables, and classes defined in the module by using the module name as a prefix.

Importing Specific Functions or Variables

If you only need specific functions or variables from a module, you can selectively import them using the 'from' keyword:

```
from module_name import function_name, variable_name
```

This syntax allows you to directly use the imported functions or variables without the need for the module name prefix.

Module Aliases

You can also provide an alias for a module using the 'as' keyword. This allows you to use a shorter or more descriptive name when referencing the module in your code:

```
import module_name as alias
```

With the alias, you can use the shortened name instead of the original module name throughout your code.

Understanding module importing is crucial to harnessing the power of modules in Python and effectively utilizing their functionality in your programs.

6.1.4 Standard Library Modules

Python's standard library is a collection of modules that come bundled with the Python installation. These modules provide a wide range of functionality for various tasks, including mathematical computations, random number generation, date and time operations, file handling, network communication, and more. Leveraging the power of standard library modules can significantly simplify your coding tasks and improve your productivity.

6.1.5 Commonly Used Standard Modules

The Python standard library offers a plethora of modules, but there are a few commonly used ones that you are likely to encounter frequently. Let's explore some of these popular standard modules:

Table 6.1: *Commonly used modules of Python standard library*

Library	Functions
math module	Provides mathematical functions to support types of calculations
cmath module	Provides mathematical functions for complex numbers
random module	Provides functions for generating pseudo-random numbers
statistics module	Provides mathematical statistics functions
urllib Module	Provides URL handling functions so that you can access websites from within your program

6.1.6 Math module

The math module in Python provides a range of mathematical functions and constants. It is part of the standard library, so no additional installation is required. Here are some commonly used functions and constants from the math module:

- math.sqrt(x): Returns the square root of x.
- math.ceil(x): Returns the smallest integer greater than or equal to x.
- math.floor(x): Returns the largest integer less than or equal to x.
- math.pow(x, y): Returns x raised to the power y.
- math.exp(x): Returns e raised to the power x, where e is Euler's number (approximately 2.71828).
- math.log(x): Returns the natural logarithm (base e) of x.
- math.log10(x): Returns the base-10 logarithm of x.

- math.sin(x), math.cos(x), math.tan(x): Return the trigonometric sine, cosine, and tangent of x (in radians).
- math.radians(degrees): Converts degrees to radians.
- math.degrees(radians): Converts radians to degrees.
- math.pi: A constant representing the mathematical constant pi (approximately 3.14159).
- math.e: A constant representing Euler's number e (approximately 2.71828).

The module offers many more mathematical functions for various purposes, including trigonometry, logarithms, rounding, exponentiation, and more. You can refer to the Python documentation for a complete list of functions and further details on their usage.

6.1.7   Cmath module

The cmath module in Python provides mathematical functions for complex numbers. It is similar to the math module but specifically designed to handle complex number operations. Here are some commonly used functions and constants from the cmath module:

- cmath.sqrt(z): Returns the square root of a complex number z.
- cmath.exp(z): Returns the exponential of a complex number z.
- cmath.log(z): Returns the natural logarithm of a complex number z.
- cmath.sin(z), cmath.cos(z), cmath.tan(z): Return the trigonometric sine, cosine, and tangent of a complex number z.
- cmath.phase(z): Returns the phase angle of a complex number z, in radians.
- cmath.polar(z): Returns the polar coordinates (magnitude, phase) of a complex number z as a tuple.
- cmath.rect(r, phi): Returns a complex number with magnitude r and phase angle phi.
- cmath.isinf(z), cmath.isnan(z): Check if a complex number z is infinite or not a number (NaN).
- cmath.pi: A constant representing the mathematical constant pi (approximately 3.14159) for complex numbers.
- cmath.e: A constant representing Euler's number e (approximately 2.71828) for complex numbers.

These functions and constants provided by the cmath module are specifically designed to handle complex number operations. They allow you to perform mathematical operations like square root, exponential, logarithm, and trigonometric functions on complex numbers. You can refer to the Python documentation for a complete list of functions and further details on their usage.

6.1.8 Random module

The random module in Python provides functions for generating random numbers and making random choices. It is part of the standard library, so no additional installation is required. Here are some commonly used functions from the random module:

- random.random(): Returns a random float between 0 and 1.
- random.randint(a, b): Returns a random integer between a and b (inclusive).
- random.choice(seq): Returns a random element from a sequence seq.
- random.shuffle(seq): Shuffles (randomly reorders) the elements in a sequence seq in place.
- random.sample(population, k): Returns a random sample of k unique elements from a population.
- random.uniform(a, b): Returns a random float between a and b (inclusive).
- random.gauss(mu, sigma): Returns a random float following a Gaussian distribution with mean mu and standard deviation sigma.
- random.seed(a=None): Initializes the random number generator with a given seed value a. If no seed is provided, it uses the system time.

These are just a few examples of the functions available in the random module. The module provides a wide range of functions for generating random numbers, making random choices, shuffling sequences, and more. It also allows you to set a seed value for reproducible results. You can refer to the Python documentation for a complete list of functions and further details on their usage.

6.1.9 Statistics Module

The statistics module in Python provides functions for statistical calculations and analysis. It is part of the standard library, so no additional installation is required. Here are some commonly used functions from the statistics module:

- statistics.mean(data): Returns the arithmetic mean (average) of a sequence of numerical data.
- statistics.median(data): Returns the median (middle value) of a sequence of numerical data.
- statistics.mode(data): Returns the mode (most common value) of a sequence of data. If there are multiple modes, it returns the smallest one.
- statistics.stdev(data): Returns the sample standard deviation of a sequence of numerical data.
- statistics.variance(data): Returns the sample variance of a sequence of numerical data.
- statistics.median_high(data): Returns the high median of a sequence of numerical data. If the number of data points is odd, it returns the middle value. If the number of data points is even, it returns the larger of the two middle values.
- statistics.median_low(data): Returns the low median of a sequence of numerical data. If the number of data points is odd, it returns the middle value. If the number of data points is even, it returns the smaller of the two middle values.
- statistics.harmonic_mean(data): Returns the harmonic mean of a sequence of numerical data.
- statistics.pvariance(data): Returns the population variance of a sequence of numerical data.
- statistics.pstdev(data): Returns the population standard deviation of a sequence of numerical data.

These functions provided by the statistics module are useful for basic statistical calculations and analysis. They allow you to calculate measures of central tendency (mean, median, mode), measures of spread (standard deviation, variance), and other statistical measures. You can refer to the Python documentation for a complete list of functions and further details on their usage.

6.1.10   Urllib module

The urllib module in Python provides functions for working with URLs (Uniform Resource Locators). It is part of the standard library and offers a variety of functions for handling different aspects of URLs and making network requests. Here are some commonly used components and functions from the urllib module:

1. urllib.parse: This submodule provides functions for parsing URLs and working with URL components. Some commonly used functions include:
   - urllib.parse.urlparse(url): Parse a URL into its components (scheme, netloc, path, etc.).
   - urllib.parse.urljoin(base, url): Construct a complete URL by combining a base URL and a relative URL.
   - urllib.parse.quote(string): URL-encode special characters in a string.
2. urllib.request: This submodule allows you to make HTTP requests and handle responses. Some commonly used functions include:
   - urllib.request.urlopen(url): Open a URL and return a file-like object representing the response.
   - urllib.request.urlretrieve(url, filename): Download a file from a URL and save it to a local file.
   - urllib.request.Request(url, data=None, headers={}, method=None): Create a request object that can be customized before sending.
3. urllib.error: This submodule provides exceptions related to URL and network operations, such as URLError and HTTPError, which can be used to handle errors that occur during network requests.
4. urllib.robotparser: This submodule provides a RobotFileParser class for parsing and working with robots.txt files. It allows you to check if a specific URL is allowed or disallowed for web crawling.

These are some of the key components and functions available in the urllib module. They allow you to parse and manipulate URLs, make HTTP requests, handle responses, and work with robots.txt files. The module provides a powerful set of tools for working with web resources in Python. You can refer to the Python documentation for a more detailed explanation and further examples of usage.

The table 6.2 provides a brief overview of the purpose and functionality of each module

Table 6.2: Modules and its description

Module	Description
math	Provides mathematical functions and constants.
random	Offers functions for generating random numbers and making random choices.
datetime	Allows manipulation and formatting of dates and times.
os	Provides functions for interacting with the operating system.
sys	Contains system-specific parameters and functions.
json	Enables parsing and generating JSON data.
csv	Provides functionality for reading and writing CSV files.
re	Offers regular expression operations for pattern matching.
requests	Simplifies making HTTP requests.
sqlite3	Provides an interface to work with SQLite databases.
pickle	Enables object serialization.
argparse	Simplifies command-line argument parsing.
logging	Provides a logging framework for recording log messages.
time	Allows working with time-related functions.
collections	Offers additional data structures beyond the built-in ones.
urllib	Provides functions for working with URLs.
statistics	Offers functions for statistical calculations and analysis.
cmath	Provides mathematical functions for complex numbers.
urllib.parse	Allows parsing and working with URL components.
urllib.request	Provides functions for making HTTP requests and handling responses.
urllib.error	Contains exceptions related to URL and network operations.
urllib.robotparser	Allows parsing and working with **robots.txt** files.

6.2   Exploring Standard Library Documentation

The Python standard library is extensive, containing numerous modules covering diverse areas of functionality. To explore and utilize these modules effectively, it is essential to consult the official Python documentation.

The Python documentation provides detailed information about each standard library module, including its purpose, available functions, classes, and constants, as well as usage examples. The documentation also highlights any considerations, limitations, or additional dependencies associated with each module.

The official Python documentation is available online at https://docs.python.org/, and it serves as a valuable resource for understanding and harnessing the power of the standard library modules. Familiarizing yourself with the documentation will empower you to leverage the standard library modules to their full potential in your Python projects.

By leveraging the functionality provided by standard library modules, you can save time and effort in implementing common tasks and focus more on solving the core problems at hand.

6.3 Creating and Using Custom Modules

In addition to utilizing the modules provided by the Python standard library, you can create your own custom modules to encapsulate related code and create reusable components. Creating custom modules allows you to modularize your own code and promote code organization and reusability.

6.3.1 Creating a Module

To create a custom module, you need to define a Python script containing the desired functionality. Here are the steps to create a module:

1. Create a new Python script with a '.py' extension.
2. Write the desired code, including variable definitions, function declarations, and class definitions, within the script.
3. Save the script with an appropriate name that reflects the module's purpose.

For example, let's say you want to create a module called 'utils' that contains various utility functions. You would create a file called 'utils.py' and define your utility functions within that script.

6.3.2 Importing Custom Modules

Once you have created a custom module, you can import it into your Python program to make use of its functionality. The process of importing a custom module is similar to importing a standard library module.

To import a custom module, follow these steps:

1. Ensure that the custom module is located in the same directory as your program, or in a directory included in the Python module search path (discussed in the next subsection).
2. Use the 'import' statement followed by the name of the module without the '.py' extension.

For example, to import the 'utils' module we created earlier, you can use the following import statement:

```
import utils
```

Once imported, you can access the functions, variables, or classes defined in the custom module using the module name as a prefix. For example, if the 'utils' module contains a function called

```
'calculate average()', you can call it as 'utils.calculateaverage()'.
```

6.3.3 Module Search Path

When importing modules, Python searches for the module files in specific directories. This set of directories is collectively known as the module search path. Understanding how Python searches for modules can help you ensure that your custom modules are accessible to your programs.

By default, Python searches for modules in the following locations:
1. The current directory (the directory from which the script is executed).
2. Directories specified in the 'PYTHONPATH' environment variable.
3. Standard library directories.

To ensure that your custom module can be imported, you can place it in one of these directories or add the directory containing the module to the 'PYTHON PATH' environment variable.

6.3.4 Package Importing

In addition to individual modules, Python allows you to organize related modules into packages. A package is a directory that contains multiple modules and an additional file called 'init.py'. Packages provide a hierarchical structure for organizing modules and help avoid naming conflicts.

To import a module from a package, you can use the 'import' statement with the package name and module name separated by a dot. For example, to import a module called 'module name' from a package called 'package name', you would use:

```
import package_name.module_name
```

This syntax allows you to access the module within the package using the package name as a prefix.

Creating and using custom modules gives you the flexibility to organize and reuse your own code effectively. By creating modular and reusable components, you can streamline your development process and enhance the maintainability of your Python projects.

6.4 Module Organizational Techniques

Organizing your modules effectively is crucial for maintaining a clean and manageable codebase. This section covers various techniques for organizing and structuring your modules, including namespace and scoping, module documentation, and module-level constants.

6.4.1 Namespace and Scoping

Modules provide a separate namespace for the code they contain, helping avoid naming conflicts. It's important to understand how namespaces and scoping work within modules to ensure proper code organization and prevent unintended consequences.

By default, when you define variables, functions, or classes within a module, they are accessible only within that module's namespace. However, you can choose to expose specific components of a module's namespace by using the 'from' statement or by explicitly importing them.

Using proper scoping techniques within modules helps encapsulate and pro- tect your code, preventing unintended modifications or name clashes. It's good practice to limit the exposure of variables, functions, and classes to only what is necessary and clearly document the intended usage of each component.

6.4.2 Module Documentation

Documentation is a crucial aspect of maintaining and sharing modules. Well- documented modules provide clear explanations of their purpose, functionality, and usage, making it easier for others (including yourself) to understand and utilize the module.

To document your modules effectively, you can include comments and doc- strings within your code. Comments provide brief explanations of code segments, while docstrings are multi-line strings that provide detailed documentation for functions, classes, and modules.

Python has a built-in documentation system that allows you to generate documentation from docstrings using tools like Sphinx or by utilizing the 'help()' function within the Python interpreter.

By documenting your modules thoroughly, you make them more accessible and user-friendly, promoting collaboration and ensuring the long-term maintainability of your code.

6.4.3   Module-Level Constants

Module-level constants are variables that hold values that remain constant throughout the module's execution. They are typically defined at the top of a module and can be accessed by all functions and classes within the module.

Using module-level constants improves code readability, as it provides a clear indication of values that should not be modified. Additionally, it allows for easy modification of constants across the entire module by changing their value at a single location.

When defining module-level constants, it's good practice to use uppercase names to differentiate them from variables and clearly indicate their purpose.

6.4.4   Module Best Practices

Following best practices when working with modules ensures that your code remains maintainable, readable, and reusable. This section covers some essential best practices for modules, including naming conventions and module testing and documentation.

6.4.5   Naming Conventions

Using consistent and meaningful names for your modules is essential for code readability and maintainability. Follow these naming conventions to ensure clarity:
- Choose descriptive and self-explanatory names for your modules that reflect their purpose.
- Use lowercase letters and underscores to separate words in module names.

- Avoid using names that conflict with Python keywords or built-in functions.

By adhering to naming conventions, you make it easier for yourself and others to understand and work with your modules.

6.5 Module Testing and Documentation

To ensure the quality and reliability of your modules, it's crucial to test them thoroughly and document their usage and behavior.

Write unit tests to verify that your module functions and classes perform as expected in different scenarios. By incorporating testing frameworks such as 'unittest' or 'pytest', you can automate the testing process and catch any potential issues early.

Additionally, document your modules using docstrings and comments, as discussed earlier. Provide clear explanations of the module's purpose, parameters, return values, and any limitations or assumptions. This documentation helps users understand how to use your module effectively and aids in troubleshooting and debugging.

6.6 Conclusion

Modules are a powerful organizational tool in Python, allowing you to encapsulate related code, promote reusability, and enhance code maintainability. By leveraging module organizational techniques, such as namespaces, proper scoping, documentation, and constant usage, you can create clean, well-structured modules that facilitate collaboration and efficient development.

Adhering to module best practices, including naming conventions, thorough testing, and comprehensive documentation, ensures that your modules are reliable, easy to understand, and ready for reuse in various projects.

By incorporating these techniques and best practices into your module development workflow, you can harness the full potential of modules in Python and elevate your programming skills to the next level.

6.7 Use Case (Array)

An array is a collection of elements of the same type that are stored in contiguous memory locations. Array aren't built-in data structures in Python like Lists therefore need to be imported via the array module in order to be used.

Example 1: Creating an Array

To create an array in Python, you need to import the array module and specify the type of elements in the array. Here's an example:

```
from array import array
my_array = array('i', [1, 2, 3, 4, 5])
print(my_array)
Output:
array('i', [1, 2, 3, 4, 5])
```

In this example, we create an array named my array of type i (integer) with the initial values [1, 2, 3, 4, 5].

Example 2: Accessing Elements

You can access individual elements of an array by using their index. The index starts from 0 for the first element. Here's an example:

```
print(my_array[0])
# Output: 1
print(my_array[3])
# Output: 4
```

In this example, we access and print the value at index 0 and index 3 of the my array.

Example 3: Modifying Elements

You can modify the elements of an array by assigning new values to specific indices. Here's an example:

```
my_array[2] = 10
print(my_array)
# Output: array('i', [1, 2, 10, 4, 5])
```

In this example, we modify the value at index 2 of the my array and print the updated array.

Example 4: Array Length

You can determine the length of an array using the len() function. Here's an example:

```
length = len(my_array)
print(length)
# Output: 5
```

In this example, we calculate and print the length of the my array.

Example 5: Array Methods

The array module provides various methods to manipulate arrays. Here's an example using the append() method:

```
my_array.append(6)
print(my_array)
# Output: array('i', [1, 2, 10, 4, 5, 6])
```

In this example, we use the append() method to add an element to the end of the my array and print the updated array.

Summary:

1. Modules in Python are self-contained units of code that allow for organization and reusability.
2. They can contain variables, functions, classes, and other components.
3. There are built-in modules, third-party modules, custom modules, package modules, and namespace packages.
4. Benefits of using modules include code organization, modularity, and namespace isolation.
5. Module importing can be done using import, from, and aliases.
6. Standard library modules offer various functionalities like math, random, datetime, os, sys, urllib, statistics, etc.
7. Python's official documentation is a valuable resource for exploring standard library modules.

8. Custom modules can be created and imported for code organization and reusability.
9. Modules should follow proper naming conventions, namespace and scoping, and be well-documented.
10. Module-level constants improve readability and maintainability.
11. Testing and documentation are essential for ensuring module quality and usability.

Multiple Choice Questions (MCQ)

1. What are modules in Python?
   a) Built-in functions
   b) Self-contained units of code
   c) Data structures
   d) Operating system commands
2. Which type of module can be installed using package managers like pip?
   a) Built-in modules
   b) Third-party modules
   c) Custom modules
   d) Package modules
3. What is the purpose of a namespace in modules?
   a) To create complex data structures
   b) To store variables globally
   c) To encapsulate related code and avoid naming conflicts
   d) To manage file I/O operations
4. How is a specific function imported from a module in Python?
   a) import module_name.function_name
   b) from module_name import function_name
   c) include module_name.function_name
   d) import function_name from module_name
5. Which module in Python provides functions for mathematical calculations with complex numbers?
   a) math
   b) random
   c) statistics
   d) cmath

Short Answer Questions:

1. What are the benefits of using modules in Python?
2. Explain the difference between a custom module and a package module.
3. How can you organize related modules into a package?
4. What is the purpose of module-level constants?
5. How can you ensure that a custom module is accessible for import in your Python program?
6. What is the role of documentation in modules?
7. How does Python handle namespace isolation within modules?
8. What is the purpose of the __init__.py file in packages?
9. How can you import a module from a package?
10. How can unit testing enhance the quality of your modules?

Answer Key

1. B), Self-contained units of code
2. D), Third-party modules
3. C), To encapsulate related code and avoid naming conflicts
4. B), from module_name import function_name
5. B), cmath

DATA STRUCTURES

"Python is a clear and powerful object-oriented programming language, comparable to Perl, Ruby, Scheme, or Java." - Guido van Rossum

Introduction

Data structures are fundamental concepts in programming that allow us to efficiently store, organize, and manipulate data. They serve as the building blocks for creating complex and sophisticated programs.

In this chapter, we will explore various essential data structures in Python. We will discuss lists, tuples, sets, dictionaries, and comprehensions. Each of these data structures has its own unique characteristics, use cases, and advantages. By the end of this chapter, you will have a solid foundation in working with these data structures and will be equipped to choose the appropriate one for your specific programming needs.

In Python, data structures can be classified into two main categories: built-in data structures and user-defined data structures, as shown in figure. 7.1

7.1   Built-in Data Structures:

Python provides several built-in data structures that are readily available for use without the need for any additional libraries or modules. These built-in data structures include:

List: List is the dynamic mutable array that stores the heterogeneous data items. The list is the ordered collections of elements. It can store elements of different types and allow for dynamic resizing, insertion, deletion, and modification of elements The most common methods of lists are append (), sort(), reverse(), remove(), pop(), insert(), extend() etc. The elements of the list are accessed by integer indices, (default value is 0).

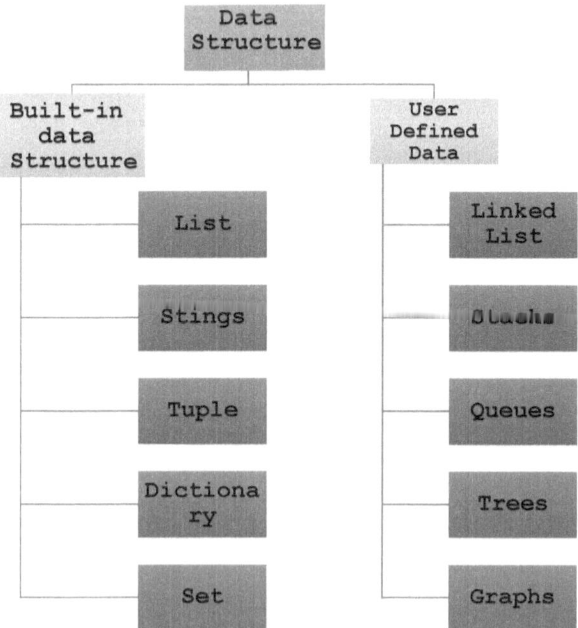

Figure 7.1: Data structures in Python

Tuple: Tuples are similar to lists, but they are immutable, meaning their elements cannot be changed after creation. Tuples are commonly used to store related values as a single entity.

Dictionary: Dictionaries are key-value pairs that provide a way to store and retrieve data based on unique keys. They are unordered and allow for efficient lookup operations.

Sets: Sets are unordered collections of unique elements. They are useful for performing set operations such as union, intersection, and difference.

7.2 User-defined Data Structures:

Python also allows users to define their own data structures by creating classes. These user-defined data structures can have custom attributes and methods, providing flexibility and abstraction in representing complex data.

Some common examples of user-defined data structures include:

- **Linked Lists**: Linked lists consist of nodes, where each node contains a value and a reference to the next node. They are dynamic data structures that allow efficient insertion and deletion at any position.

- **Stacks**: Stacks follow the Last-In-First-Out (LIFO) principle. Elements can be pushed onto the stack or popped from the stack.
- **Queues**: Queues follow the First-In-First-Out (FIFO) principle. Elements can be added to the rear (enqueue) and removed from the front (dequeue) of the queue.
- **Trees**: Trees are hierarchical data structures with a root node and child nodes. They are used for representing hierarchical relationships between elements.
- **Graphs**: Graphs consist of nodes connected by edges. They are used to represent complex relationships and can be directed or undirected.

User-defined data structures provide a way to represent and manipulate data in a manner specific to the problem domain.

Throughout this chapter, we will provide clear explanations, practical examples, and hands-on exercises to solidify your understanding of these data structures. By the end of this chapter, you will have gained the necessary knowledge and skills to leverage the power of data structures in your Python programs.

7.3   Lists

A list in Python is a versatile data structure that allows you to store and manipulate a collection of elements. It is an ordered collection, meaning the elements are stored in a specific order and can be accessed by their position or index. Lists can contain elements of different types, such as numbers, strings, booleans, and even other lists.

Lists are mutable, which means you can modify their elements. You can add or remove elements, change the value of existing elements, or reorder the elements within a list. This flexibility makes lists a powerful tool for storing and manipulating data in Python.

To create a list, you enclose the elements in square brackets ([]), separating them with commas.

Example 1: Creating a List

Here's an example of creating a list in Python:

```
my_list = [1, 2, 3, 4, 5]
```

```
print(my_list)
Output:
[1, 2, 3, 4, 5]
```

In this example, we create a list named my list with the initial values [1, 2, 3, 4, 5].

Example 2: Accessing and Modifying Elements

To access elements in a list, you can use the index, similar to arrays. Lists also support negative indexing, where -1 refers to the last element. Here's an example:

```
print(my_list[0])
# Output: 1
print(my_list[-1])
# Output: 5
my_list[2] = 10
# Modifying the third element print(my_list)
# Output: [1, 2, 10, 4, 5]
```

In this example, we access and print the value at index 0 and index -1 of the my list. We also modify the value at index 2 and print the updated list.

Example 3: List Length

You can determine the length of a list using the len() function. Here's an example:

```
length = len(my_list)
print(length)
# Output: 5
```

In this example, we calculate and print the length of the my list.

Example 4: List Methods

Lists in Python come with several built-in methods to manipulate and perform operations on the list. Here's an example using the append() method:

```
my_list.append(6)
print(my_list)
# Output: [1, 2, 10, 4, 5, 6]
```

In this example, we use the append() method to add an element to the end of the my list and print the updated list.

Example 5: List Slicing

You can slice a list to extract a portion of it. Here's an example:

```
sliced_list = my_list[1:4]
print(sliced_list)
# Output: [2, 10, 4]
```

In this example, we slice the my list from index 1 to index 3 (exclusive) and print the sliced portion.

7.4   Tuples

A tuple is another commonly used data structure in Python. It is similar to a list but has one key difference: tuples are immutable, meaning their elements cannot be modified once created. Tuples are typically used to store a collection of related values that should not be changed.

Creating a Tuple

To create a tuple in Python, you enclose the elements in parentheses () or use the built-in tuple() function. Here's an example:

```
my_tuple = (1, 2, 3, "apple", "banana") print(my_tuple)
# Output: (1, 2, 3, "apple", "banana")
```

In this example, my tuple is a tuple that contains elements of different types: integers (1, 2, 3), and strings ("apple", "banana").

Accessing Elements

Similar to lists, you can access elements in a tuple using their index. Tuples also support negative indexing, where -1 refers to the last element. Here's an example:

```python
print(my_tuple[0])
# Output: 1 print(my_tuple[-1])
# Output: "Banana"
```

In this example, we access and print the value at index 0 and index -1 of the my tuple.

Tuple Packing and Unpacking

In Python, you can pack multiple values into a tuple using a single assignment statement. Here's an example:

```python
my_tuple = 1, 2, 3
print(my_tuple)
# Output: (1, 2, 3)
```

In this example, we assign multiple values to my tuple without explicitly using parentheses. Python automatically creates a tuple with the provided values. You can also unpack a tuple by assigning its elements to individual variables.

Here's an example:

```python
x, y, z = my_tuple
print(x)
# Output:1
print(y)
# Output:2
print(z)
# Output:3
```

In this example, we unpack the values from my tuple and assign them to variables x, y, and z.

Tuple Methods

Tuples are immutable, so they do not provide methods for modifying their elements. However, they offer a few methods for operations such as counting occurrences and finding indices. Some of the commonly used methods for tuples include count() and index().

Tuples are immutable data structures in Python that allow you to store an ordered collection of elements. While similar to lists, tuples cannot be modified once created, making them suitable for storing fixed data or related values. You can access tuple elements, pack and unpack values, and utilize tuple methods for operations on tuples.

7.5   Dictionaries

A dictionary is a powerful data structure in Python that allows you to store and retrieve data using key-value pairs. Unlike lists and tuples, which are indexed by integers, dictionaries are indexed by unique keys. This makes dictionaries a suitable choice when you want to associate data with specific identifiers or labels.

Creating a Dictionary

To create a dictionary in Python, you enclose key-value pairs in curly braces {}. Each key-value pair is separated by a colon (:). Here's an example:

```
my_dict = {"name": "John", "age": 25, "city": "New York"}
print(my_dict)
Output:
{"name": "John", "age": 25, "city": "New York"}
```

In this example, my dict is a dictionary that contains key-value pairs representing a person's name, age, and city.

Accessing and Modifying Values

You can access the value associated with a specific key in a dictionary by using the key inside square brackets. Here's an example:

```
print(my_dict["name"])
# Output: "John"
print(my_dict["age"])
```

```
# Output: 25
```

In this example, we access and print the values associated with the keys "name" and "age".

You can also modify the value associated with a key by assigning a new value to it. Here's an example:

```
my_dict["city"] = "San Francisco"
print(my_dict["city"])
# Output: "San Francisco"
```

In this example, we change the value associated with the key "city" to "San Francisco" and print the updated value.

Dictionary Methods

Dictionaries in Python come with a variety of built-in methods that allow you to manipulate and perform operations on dictionaries. Some commonly used methods include keys(), values(), items(), get(), pop(), update(), and more. These methods provide convenient ways to retrieve keys, values, and key-value pairs, add or remove items, and update dictionaries.

In summary, dictionaries are key-value pairs in Python that provide an efficient way to store and retrieve data based on unique identifiers. With dictionaries, you can create, access, modify, and perform various operations on key-value pairs, making them a powerful tool for organizing and managing data in Python.

7.6   Sets

A set is a versatile data structure in Python that represents an unordered collection of unique elements. Unlike lists or tuples, sets do not allow duplicate values, and the order of elements is not guaranteed. Sets are useful when you want to work with a collection of items without any specific ordering or need to eliminate duplicates.

Creating a Set

To create a set in Python, you enclose elements in curly braces {}. Alternatively, you can use the built-in set() function. Here's an example:

```
my_set = {1, 2, 3, 4, 5}
print(my_set)
Output: {1, 2, 3, 4, 5}
```

In this example, my set is a set that contains unique elements: 1, 2, 3, 4, and 5.

Operations on Sets

Sets in Python support a variety of operations such as union, intersection, difference, and symmetric difference. These operations allow you to combine, compare, and manipulate sets.

Here's an example that demonstrates some common set operations:

```
set1 = {1, 2, 3, 4, 5}
set2 = {4, 5, 6, 7, 8}
union = set1.union(set2)
print(union)
# Output: {1, 2, 3, 4, 5, 6, 7, 8}
intersection = set1.intersection(set2)
print(intersection)
# Output: {4, 5}
difference = set1.difference(set2)
print(difference)
# Output: {1, 2, 3}
symmetric_difference = set1.symmetric_difference(set2)
print(symmetric_difference)
# Output: {1, 2, 3, 6, 7, 8}
```

In this example, we create two sets (set1 and set2) and perform various operations such as union, intersection, difference, and symmetric difference.

Set Methods

Sets in Python come with a variety of built-in methods that allow you to perform operations on sets. Some commonly used set methods include add(), remove(), discard(), pop(), clear(), and more. These methods provide convenient ways to add or remove elements from sets, retrieve elements, or perform set operations. Sets in Python are unordered collections of unique elements that provide efficient ways to eliminate duplicates and perform set operations. With sets, you can create, manipulate, and perform operations such as union, intersection, and difference, making them valuable tool for data manipulation and set theory operations.

Summary

In Python, there are several fundamental data structures that are commonly used for organizing and manipulating data. Here's a brief summary of the key data structures:

Lists: Lists are ordered collections of elements that can be of different types. They are mutable, meaning their elements can be modified. Lists are created using square brackets and can be accessed, modified, and operated upon using various list methods.

Tuples: Tuples are similar to lists but are immutable, meaning their elements cannot be modified once created. Tuples are created using parentheses or the tuple() function. They are often used to store related values that should not be changed.

Dictionaries: Dictionaries are unordered collections of key-value pairs. They provide a way to associate data with specific identifiers or labels. Dictionaries are created using curly braces or the dict () function. They are widely used for fast data retrieval based on unique keys.

Sets: Sets are unordered collections of unique elements. They do not allow duplicate values. Sets are created using curly braces or the set() function. They are useful for performing set operations such as union, intersection, and difference.

These data structures offer different functionalities and are chosen based on specific needs. Understanding their characteristics and operations can greatly enhance data organization and manipulation in Python programming.

Examples Involving Lists in Python

Example

You are given a list of numbers. Write a function in Python to find the maximum value in the list.

```
def find_max(numbers): return max(numbers)
numbers = [10, 5, 20, 15, 30] print(find_max(numbers))
```

Example

Write a Python program to remove all duplicate elements from a given list and print the updated list.

```python
def remove_duplicates(lst): return list(set(lst))
my_list = [1, 2, 3, 3, 4, 5, 5, 6]
print(remove_duplicates(my_list))
```

Example

You are given two lists, list1 and list2. Write a Python program to combine the two lists into a single list without any duplicate elements.

```python
def combine_lists(list1, list2): combined_list = list(set(list1 + list2))
return combined_list
list1 = [1, 2, 3, 4]
list2 = [3, 4, 5, 6]
print(combine_lists(list1, list2))
```

Example

Write a Python function to check if a given list is sorted in ascending order.

```python
def is_sorted(lst):
return all(lst[i] <= lst[i+1] for i in range(len(lst)-1))
numbers = [1, 2, 3, 4, 5] print(is_sorted(numbers))
```

Example

You are given a list of strings. Write a Python program to count the number of strings in the list that have a length greater than 5.

```python
def count_long_strings(lst):
return len([s for s in lst if len(s) > 5])
words = ["apple", "banana", "grapefruit", "kiwi", "orange"] print(count_
long_strings
```

Multiple-Choice Questions (MCQs)

1. What is a key characteristic of tuples in Python?
   a) They allow duplicate elements.
   b) They are mutable.
   c) They are unordered.
   d) They are immutable.

2. Which data structure in Python is suitable for performing set operations like union and intersection?
   a) Lists
   b) Tuples
   c) Dictionaries
   d) Sets

3. Which data structure is used for storing a collection of key-value pairs in Python?
   a) Arrays
   b) Sets
   c) Lists
   d) Dictionaries

4. What does the "append()" method do in Python lists?
   a) Removes an element from the list.
   b) Adds an element to the beginning of the list.
   c) Adds an element to the end of the list.
   d) Sorts the list in ascending order.

5. Which data structure in Python is similar to a list but does not allow duplicate elements?
   a) Tuples
   b) Dictionaries
   c) Sets
   d) Arrays

6. What is the main advantage of using dictionaries in Python?
   a) They maintain the order of elements.
   b) They allow duplicate keys.

c) They provide fast data retrieval based on keys.
d) They allow mutable values.

7. Which operation can be used to combine two sets in Python?
   a) Addition
   b) Union
   c) Concatenation
   d) Intersection

8. Which method can be used to remove an element from a Python list?
   a) remove()
   b) discard()
   c) delete()
   d) exclude()

9. In Python, what data structure would you use if you need an ordered collection of elements that can be modified?
   a) Tuples
   b) Sets
   c) Arrays
   d) Lists

10. What is the key difference between a list and a tuple in Python?
    a) Lists are immutable, while tuples are mutable.
    b) Tuples allow duplicate elements, while lists do not.
    c) Lists are ordered, while tuples are unordered.
    d) Lists can store elements of different types, while tuples cannot.

Short Answer Questions

1. Explain the main difference between lists and tuples in Python.
2. Describe two advantages of using dictionaries in Python.
3. Write a Python function to find the intersection of two sets.
4. How can you access the value associated with a specific key in a dictionary?
5. Provide an example of using the "append()" method to add an element to a Python list.
6. What is the purpose of using the "union()" method on sets in Python?

7. How can you determine the length of a given list in Python?
8. Write a brief explanation of the purpose of the "difference()" method in sets.
9. What is the significance of the "symmetric_difference()" method when working with sets?
10. Explain the concept of "unpacking" when dealing with tuples in Python.

Answer Key

1. d) They are immutable.
2. d) Sets
3. d) Dictionaries
4. c) Adds an element to the end of the list.
5. c) Sets
6. c) They provide fast data retrieval based on keys.
7. b) Union
8. a) remove()
9. d) Lists
10. b) Tuples allow duplicate elements, while lists do not.

FILE HANDLING

"Python is an experiment in how much freedom programmers need. Too much freedom and nobody can read another's code; too little and expressiveness is endangered." - Guido van Rossum

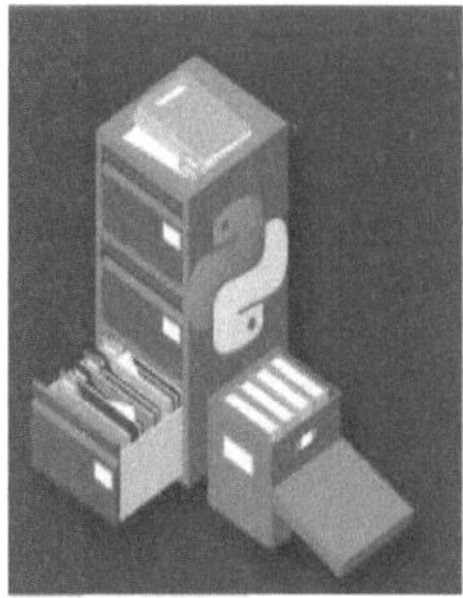

In this chapter, we will explore various aspects of file handling in Python. File handling is an essential concept in programming that allows us to interact with files stored on a computer's filesystem. It enables us to read data from files, write data to files, and perform other file-related operations. Figure 8.1 shows file handling operations in python.

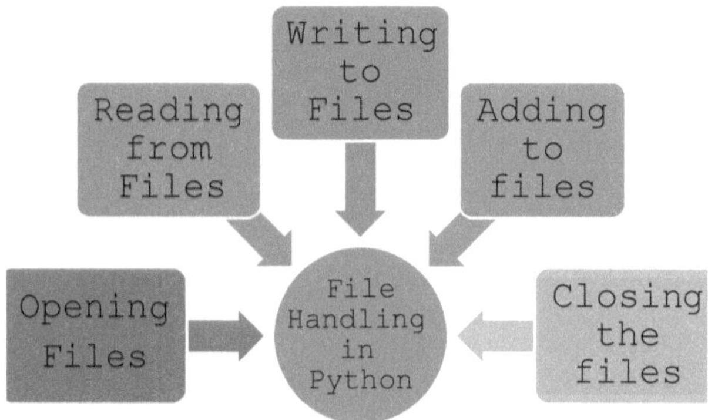

Figure 8.1: File Handling in Python

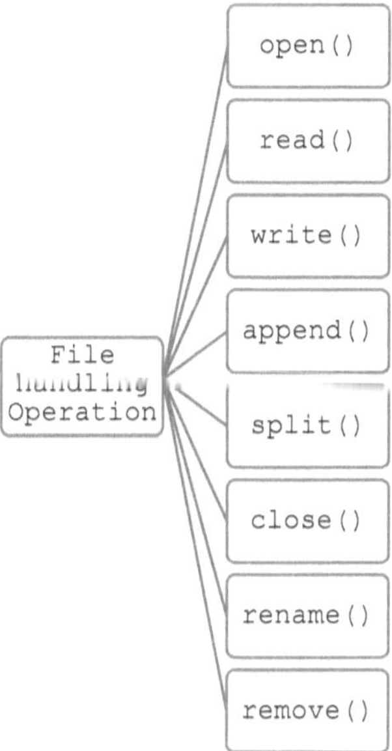

Figure 8.2: File Handling operations in Python

8.1   Opening and Closing Files

One of the fundamental steps in file handling is opening a file, shown in figure 8.2. In Python, we can use the open() function to open a file. The open() function takes two arguments: the filename and the mode in which the file should be opened. The mode can be one of the following:

- 'r': read mode (default)
- 'w': write mode (overwrites the file if it exists)
- 'a': append mode (appends data to the end of the file)
- 'x': exclusive creation mode (creates a new file, but raises an error if it already exists)

Here's an example that demonstrates opening a file in read mode and printing its contents:

```
file = open("example.txt", "r")
content = file.read()
print(content)
file.close()
```

Closing a file is important to release the system resources used by the file.

In Python, we can use the close() method to close a file. It is good practice to always close a file after we are done with it to free up resources and avoid potential issues.

9.2   Reading and Writing Text Files

Text files contain human-readable text. Python provides different methods to read and write text files. To read the contents of a text file, we can use the read() or readline() methods. The read() method reads the entire contents of the file as a string, while the readline() method reads a single line from the file. Here's an example that demonstrates reading a text file line by line:

```
file = open ("example.txt", "r") for line in file: print(line) file.
close().
```

To write data to a text file, we can use the write() method or the writelines() method. The write() method writes a string to the file, while the writelines() method writes a list of strings to the file. Here's an example that demonstrates writing data to a text file:

```
file = open("example.txt", "w")
file.write("Hello, World!")
file.close()
```

9.3   Reading and Writing Binary Files

Binary files contain non-textual data, such as images, audio, or video. Python supports reading and writing binary files using the rb (read binary) and wb (write binary) modes, respectively.

To read binary data from a file, we can use the read() method with the appropriate mode. Here's an example that demonstrates reading a binary file and writing its content to a new file:

```
with open("input.jpg", "rb") as input_file:
data = input_file.read()
with open("output.jpg", "wb") as output_file:
output_file.write(data)
```

To write binary data to a file, we can use the write() method with the appropriate mode. Here's an example that demonstrates writing binary data to a file:

```
data = b'\x48\x65\x6c\x6c\x6f\x2c\x20\x57\x6f\x72\x6c\x64\x21'
with open("output.bin", "wb") as file:
file.write(data)
```

9.4 Exception Handling in File Operations

File operations can raise exceptions, such as when a file does not exist or when there are permission issues. To handle these exceptions, we can use the try-except block. By using exception handling, we can gracefully handle errors and prevent our program from crashing.

Here's an example that demonstrates exception handling when opening a file:

```
try:
file = open("example.txt", "r")
content = file.read()
print(content)
file.close()
except FileNotFoundError:
print("File not found!")
except PermissionError:
print("Permission denied!")
```

Advantages of File Handling:

1. **Data Persistence**: Files provide a means of storing data persistently on a computer's filesystem. They allow data to be stored even after the program has finished executing, ensuring that the data is available for future use.

2. **Data Sharing**: Files can be easily shared between different programs and systems. They provide a common and standardized format for data exchange, allowing seamless integration between different applications.

3. **Large Data Storage**: Files offer the ability to store and manage large amounts of data. They can handle data of varying sizes, ranging from a few bytes to several gigabytes or more, making them suitable for storing complex and extensive datasets.

4. **Random Access**: Files allow random access to data, meaning that specific portions of the file can be accessed and modified directly without the need to read or modify the entire file. This random access capability enables efficient data retrieval and manipulation.

5. **Data Integrity**: Files provide mechanisms to ensure the integrity and consistency of data. File systems often incorporate features such as file permissions, file locking, and file versioning to protect data from unauthorized access, concurrent modifications, or accidental data loss.

Disadvantages of File Handling:

1. **Performance Overhead**: File operations, especially with large files or frequent read/write operations, can introduce performance overhead. Disk I/O operations are typically slower compared to operations performed in memory, which can impact the overall performance of the program.

2. **Limited Concurrency**: File systems often impose limitations on concurrent access to files. Multiple processes or threads attempting to access the same file simultaneously can result in conflicts, such as data corruption or inconsistent states. Proper synchronization mechanisms are required to handle concurrency issues.

3. **File Management**: Handling files involves managing their creation, deletion, and organization. It is the responsibility of the programmer to ensure proper file management, including error handling, cleanup, and resource deallocation. Improper file management can lead to resource leaks and potential data loss.

4. **Platform Dependence**: File handling can be platform-dependent, as different operating systems may have varying file system structures, file path conventions, or file access permissions. Programs relying heavily on file handling may require additional considerations and adaptations to ensure cross-platform compatibility.

5. **Security Risks**: Files can be susceptible to security risks, such as unauthorized access, file tampering, or malware injection. Proper security measures, such as file encryption, user authentication, and input validation, should be implemented to mitigate these risks.

Here's an example that demonstrates implementing various functions in file handling, including open(), with(), split(), and append()

```python
# Using open() function to open a file in write mode
file = open("example.txt", "w")
file.write("Hello, World!")
file.close()
# Using with statement to open a file in read mode
with open("example.txt", "r") as file:
content = file.read()
print(content)
# Using split() function to split the content of the file into words
words = content.split()
print(words)
# Using append() function to add more content to the file
with open("example.txt", "a") as file:
file.write("\nThis is additional content.")
```

Explanation:

1. First, we open a file named "example.txt" in write mode using the open() function. We write the string "Hello, World!" to the file and then close it.
2. Next, we use the with statement to open the same file in read mode. We read the contents of the file using the read() method and store it in the content variable.
3. We then split the content of the file into a list of words using the split() method and store it in the words variable.
4. Finally, we open the file in append mode using the with statement and add the string "This is additional content." to the file using the write() method.

This example showcases the usage of different functions in file handling, including opening a file, using the with statement for automatic file handling, splitting the file content into words, and appending additional content to the file.

Summary

File handling is a crucial aspect of programming that involves interacting with files on a computer's filesystem. Python offers versatile tools to facilitate file operations. Opening files is done with the open() function, and it's essential to close files using the close() method to free up resources. Text files, containing human-readable content, can be read line by line using the readline() method and written to using the write() method. Binary files, containing non-textual data, can be read using the rb mode and written using the wb mode. Exception handling, implemented through try-except blocks, is crucial for gracefully handling file-related errors.

Advantages of file handling include data persistence, sharing, large data storage, random access, and data integrity. However, there are challenges like performance overhead, limited concurrency, file management, platform dependence, and security risks.

MCQs:

1. What is the default mode when opening a file using open()?
   a) 'w'
   b) 'a'
   c) 'x'
   d) 'r'
2. Which method reads a single line from a text file?
   a) read()
   b) readlines()
   c) readline()
   d) readLine()
3. Which mode is used to open a file for binary reading?
   a) br
   b) rb
   c) binary_read
   d) read_binary
4. Which function is essential to free up system resources after file usage?
   a) release()
   b) close()
   c) clear()
   d) free()
5. Which advantage of file handling makes it suitable for storing images?
   a) Data Persistence
   b) Large Data Storage

   c) Data Sharing

   d) Random Access

6. Which method is used to write a string to a text file?

   a) append()

   b) add()

   c) insert()

   d) write()

7. What is a primary reason to use exception handling in file operations?

   a) To make the code complex

   b) To avoid using the open() function

   c) To prevent the program from crashing

   d) To skip the try block

8. Which mode creates a new file but raises an error if it already exists?

   a) x

   b) w

   c) a

   d) r

9. Which disadvantage of file handling is associated with slower read/write operations?

   a) Limited Concurrency

   b) Performance Overhead

   c) File Management

   d) Security Risks

10. What is a key characteristic of binary files?

   a) They contain human-readable text

   b) They support the "x" mode

   c) They are opened using the "rb" mode

   d) They can be modified using text editors

ANSWER KEY

1. d) 'r'

2. c) readline()

3. b) rb

4. b) close()

5. b) Large Data Storage

6. d) write()

7. c) To prevent the program from crashing
8. a) x
9. b) Performance Overhead
10. c) They are opened using the "rb" mode

SHORT ANSWER QUESTIONS

1. What is file handling in Python?
2. What are the steps involved in file handling?
3. How can you open a file in Python? Provide an example.
4. Why is it important to close a file after we are done with it?
5. How can you read the contents of a text file? Provide an example.
6. How can you write data to a text file? Provide an example.
7. What are binary files? How are they different from text files?
8. How can you read binary data from a file? Provide an example.
9. How can you write binary data to a file? Provide an example.
10. Why is exception handling important in file operations? Provide an example where exception handling is used.

OBJECT – ORIENTED PROGRAMMING

Python's seamless integration with operating systems empowers developers to interact with the underlying system, effortlessly harnessing its capabilities and resources to build powerful applications." - Unknown

Introduction to OOP

In the ever-evolving landscape of software development, Object-Oriented Programming (OOP) has emerged as a paradigm that brings structure, organization, and modularity to code. At its heart, OOP offers a new perspective on designing and building software by mirroring real-world entities and their intricate interactions. This approach not only enhances the clarity of code but also encourages the creation of reusable components, making OOP a favored methodology for tackling complexity in modern programming.

The core philosophy of OOP lies in its ability to encapsulate data and functions into cohesive units known as objects. These objects serve as building blocks, each possessing its own unique set of attributes (data) and behaviors (methods). By modeling software entities after real-world objects, developers can better represent the complexities of the problem domain. Imagine a software application that simulates a library. With OOP, the programmer can create classes such as "Book," "Author," and "Library," each equipped with relevant data (e.g., book title, author name) and actions (e.g., borrowing a book).

Python, a versatile and expressive programming language, is particularly adept at translating OOP principles into code. Its elegant syntax aligns well with the concepts of classes, objects, inheritance, and polymorphism. Python's emphasis on readability further enhances the understanding of OOP code, enabling developers to focus on the logic rather than deciphering convoluted syntax.

Throughout this chapter, we embark on a journey to uncover the essence of OOP and its manifestation in Python. By mastering OOP, you gain a powerful toolkit for constructing software that mirrors the intricacies of the real world, resulting in applications that are more organized, adaptable, and maintainable. Whether you're constructing a game engine, developing a financial system, or creating intricate simulations, the principles of OOP can guide you in crafting software solutions that reflect the richness and complexity of the environments they model.

Through a comprehensive exploration of fundamental concepts such as classes, objects, inheritance, polymorphism, encapsulation, and abstraction, you'll not only learn the mechanics of OOP but also develop a deep appreciation for its elegance and practicality. Armed with this knowledge, you'll be prepared to tackle even the most complex programming challenges, crafting software that aligns harmoniously with the world it interacts with. As we dive into the heart of OOP, its components, as shown in figure 9.1 and its implementation in Python, you'll discover how this paradigm can transform your programming endeavors into a journey of creativity, organization, and innovation.

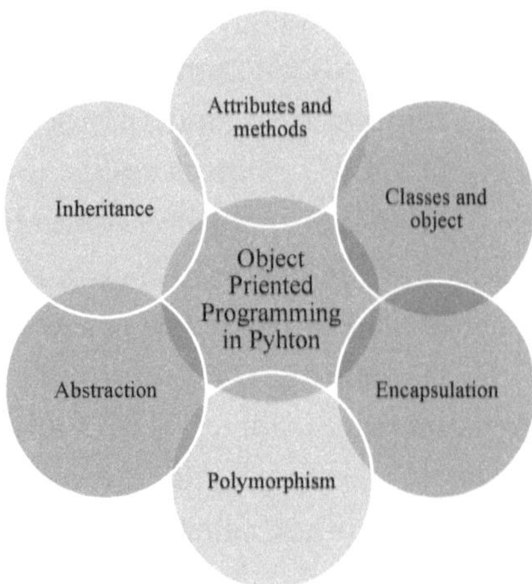

Figure 9.1: Components of Object-oriented programming in Python

9.1 Classes and Objects

At the core of Object-Oriented Programming (OOP) are two crucial concepts: classes and objects. These concepts provide a powerful way to model real-world entities and interactions within a programming framework. Let's delve deeper into these concepts with examples to illustrate their significance.

Classes: Blueprints for Objects

A class is like a blueprint that defines the structure and behavior of objects. It specifies the attributes (data) the objects will have and the methods (functions) they can perform. Think of a class as a template that describes the properties and actions an object of that class can have. For instance, let's consider a class named Person:

```python
class Person:
def __init__(self, name, age):
self.name = name
self.age = age
def greet(self):
print(f"Hello, my name is {self.name} and I am {self.age} years old.")
```

In the above example, the Person class has attributes name and age, and a method greet().

Objects: Instances of Classes

An object is an instance of a class, created based on the blueprint defined by the class. It has specific values for its attributes and can perform the methods defined in the class. Continuing with the Person class example, let's create two Person objects:

```python
person1 = Person("Alice", 30)
person2 = Person("Bob", 25)
person1.greet() # Output: Hello, my name is Alice and I am 30 years old.
person2.greet() # Output: Hello, my name is Bob and I am 25 years old.
```

Each object, person1 and person2, is an instance of the Person class, and they have their own unique attribute values.

Benefits and Significance

Classes and objects provide a structured and modular approach to programming. They allow you to encapsulate data and functionality, promoting code reusability and organization. For instance, you can create a Car class with attributes like make, model, and year, and methods like start_engine() and accelerate(). Then, you can create multiple car objects with varying attributes and behaviors, all based on the same class blueprint.

By modeling real-world entities using classes and creating objects from those classes, OOP enables you to develop complex systems that closely resemble the interactions and behaviors of the real world. This makes code more intuitive, maintainable, and adaptable as your software evolves.

Classes and objects are the fundamental building blocks of Object-Oriented Programming. They empower developers to design and implement software solutions that mirror real-world scenarios, fostering code organization, reusability, and scalability.

9.2 Attributes and Methods

When creating a class, you define its attributes and methods. Attributes represent the data associated with the class, while methods encapsulate the actions that can be performed on that data. Consider the class "Car." Its attributes might include "make," "model," and "year," while its methods could encompass "start_engine," "accelerate," and "brake."

In Python, classes are created using the class keyword. Once a class is defined, you can create objects (instances) of that class using its constructor. The constructor is a special method named __init__ that initializes the attributes of the object. For example:

```python
class Car:
    def __init__(self, make, model, year):
      self.make = make
      self.model = model
      self.year = year
def start_engine(self):
    print(f"{self.make} {self.model}'s engine started.")
my_car = Car("Toyota", "Camry", 2023)
my_car.start_engine()
```

9.3 Inheritance

Inheritance is a mechanism that allows a class to inherit the properties and behaviors of another class. It promotes code reuse and allows you to create specialized classes based on existing ones. We'll cover single and multiple inheritance, explore the concept of base and derived classes, and show you how to override methods in derived classes.

Inheritance is a cornerstone of Object-Oriented Programming that facilitates code reuse and extensibility. It allows a class (called the derived class or subclass) to inherit the attributes and methods of another class (called the base class or superclass). This promotes the creation of specialized classes while maintaining a clear hierarchy.

Example:

Consider a Shape class as the base class with a method calculate_area(). We can create specialized subclasses like Circle and Rectangle that inherit from the Shape
class:

```
class Shape:
   def calculate_area(self):
      pass
class Circle(Shape):
   def __init__(self, radius):
      self.radius = radius
def calculate_area(self):
   return 3.14 * self.radius * self.radius
class Rectangle(Shape):
   def __init__(self, width, height):
      self.width = width
      self.height = height
def calculate_area(self):
   return self.width * self.height
```

Here, both Circle and Rectangle inherit the calculate_area() method from the Shape class, and they specialize it to suit their own attributes and calculations.

9.4 Polymorphism

Polymorphism enables objects of different classes to be treated as objects of a common superclass. This concept allows for more flexible and modular code. We'll explain how to achieve polymorphism through method overriding and how to use interfaces and abstract classes to create adaptable programs.

Polymorphism allows objects of different classes to be treated as instances of a common superclass. This enables more flexible and modular code, as you can create functions that work with objects of multiple subclasses without knowing their specific types.

Example:

Let's extend the Shape example to showcase polymorphism. We'll create a function that takes a Shape object and calculates its area:

```python
def calculate_total_area(shapes):
total_area = 0
for shape in shapes:
total_area += shape.calculate_area()
return total_area
shapes = [Circle(5), Rectangle(3, 4)]
total_area = calculate_total_area(shapes)
print("Total area:", total_area)
```

The calculate_total_area() function can handle a list of different shape objects, thanks to polymorphism.

9.5   Encapsulation

Encapsulation involves bundling data (attributes) and methods (functions) that operate on that data within a single unit (a class). It promotes data protection by controlling access to attributes and keeping implementation details hidden.

Example:

Consider a BankAccount class that encapsulates the balance and provides methods to deposit and withdraw funds:

class
BankAccount:

```python
def __init__(self):
self.balance = 0
def deposit(self, amount):
if amount > 0:
self.balance += amount
def withdraw(self, amount):
if 0 < amount <= self.balance:
self.balance -= amount
def get_balance(self):
return self.balance
```

Here, the balance attribute is encapsulated within the class, and the methods provide controlled access to manipulate it.

9.6   Abstraction

Abstraction simplifies complex systems by modeling classes based on their essential attributes and behaviors. It allows you to focus on what an object does, rather than the intricate details of how it does it.

Example:

Let's abstract the concept of a Vehicle class. While we won't provide a full implementation, consider methods like start(), stop(), and get_speed(). Concrete subclasses like Car and Motorcycle would inherit from Vehicle and provide their specific implementations.

By abstracting the common functionality into a superclass and allowing subclasses to provide their own details, you create a cleaner and more organized codebase.

Examples:

This section contains examples demonstrate how to implement inheritance, polymorphism, encapsulation, and abstraction in Python programs to solve various problems in an object-oriented manner.

Inheritance: Animal Hierarchy

Problem Statement: Create a base class Animal with subclasses Dog, Cat, and Bird. Each subclass should inherit common methods from the base class while also having specific behaviors.

class Animal:

```python
def __init__(self, name):
self.name = name
def speak(self):
pass
class Dog(Animal):
def speak(self):
return f"{self.name} says Woof!"
class Cat(Animal):
def speak(self):
```

```python
return f"{self.name} says Meow!"
class Bird(Animal):
def speak(self):
return f"{self.name} says Chirp!"
# Usage
dog = Dog("Buddy")
cat = Cat("Whiskers")
bird = Bird("Tweetie")
print(dog.speak()) # Output: Buddy says Woof!
print(cat.speak()) # Output: Whiskers says Meow!
print(bird.speak()) # Output: Tweetie says Chirp!
```

Polymorphism: Shape Area Calculation

Problem Statement: Create a base class Shape with subclasses Circle and Square. Implement a function that calculates the area of any given shape.

```python
import math
class Shape:
def area(self):
pass
class Circle(Shape):
def __init__(self, radius):
self.radius = radius
def area(self):
return math.pi * self.radius ** 2
class Square(Shape):
def __init__(self, side):
self.side = side
def area(self):
return self.side ** 2
# Usage
circle = Circle(5)
square = Square(4)
print(f"Circle area: {circle.area():.2f}") # Output: Circle area: 78.54
print(f"Square area: {square.area()}") # Output: Square area: 16
```

Encapsulation: Student Information System

Problem Statement: Create a class Student that encapsulates attributes like name, age, and grades. Provide methods to update grades and calculate average.

```python
class Student:
def __init__(self, name, age):
self.name = name
self.age = age
self.grades = []
def add_grade(self, grade):
self.grades.append(grade)
def calculate_average(self):
if self.grades:
return sum(self.grades) / len(self.grades)
else:
return 0
# Usage
student1 = Student("Alice", 20)
student1.add_grade(85)
student1.add_grade(90)
student1.add_grade(78)
print(f"{student1.name}'s average grade: {student1.calculate_
average():.2f}") # Output: Alice's average grade: 84.33
```

Abstraction: Remote Control for Devices

Problem Statement: Design an abstract class RemoteControl with methods like turn_on(), turn_off(), and change_channel(). Concrete subclasses like TVRemote and ACRemote provide implementations specific to the device.

```python
from abc import ABC, abstractmethod
class RemoteControl(ABC):
@abstractmethod
def turn_on(self):
pass
@abstractmethod
def turn_off(self):
pass
@abstractmethod
def change_channel(self, channel):
pass
class TVRemote(RemoteControl):
def turn_on(self):
return "TV is turned on"
def turn_off(self):
return "TV is turned off"
```

```python
def change_channel(self, channel):
return f"TV channel changed to {channel}"
class ACRemote(RemoteControl):
def turn_on(self):
return "AC is turned on"
def turn_off(self):
return "AC is turned off"
def change_channel(self, channel):
return "AC does not have channels"
# Usage
tv_remote = TVRemote()
ac_remote = ACRemote()
print(tv_remote.turn_on())  # Output: TV is turned on
print(tv_remote.change_channel(5))  # Output: TV channel changed to 5
print(ac_remote.turn_off())  # Output: AC is turned off
print(ac_remote.change_channel(10))  # Output: AC does not have channels
```

Summary

Object-Oriented Programming is a powerful paradigm that promotes modular, reusable, and organized code. By mastering OOP concepts in Python, you'll be able to design and implement efficient and maintainable software solutions. This chapter equips you with the knowledge and tools needed to leverage the full potential of OOP in your programming journey.

Multiple Choice Questions (MCQ)

1. What is the primary goal of Object-Oriented Programming (OOP)?
   a) Minimize code complexity
   b) Optimize memory usage
   c) Model real-world entities and interactions
   d) Enhance hardware compatibility
2. In OOP, a class is best described as:
   a) An instance of an object
   b) A variable that stores data
   c) A blueprint that defines the structure and behavior of an object
   d) A mathematical equation
3. What is an object in OOP?
   a) A variable used to store values
   b) A data type in Python

c) An instance of a class, containing attributes and methods

d) A file containing Python code

4. Which OOP concept allows a class to inherit properties and behaviors from another class?

a) Encapsulation

b) Polymorphism

c) Abstraction

d) Inheritance

5. Polymorphism in OOP refers to:

a) The ability to encapsulate data

b) The ability to hide implementation details

c) The ability of different objects to be treated as instances of the same superclass

d) The ability to override methods in derived classes

6. Encapsulation in OOP involves:

a) Inheriting attributes from a parent class

b) Bundling data and methods within a class

c) Creating abstract classes

d) Using multiple inheritance

7. What does abstraction in OOP aim to achieve?

a) Modeling real-world entities

b) Hiding implementation details

c) Overriding methods in subclasses

d) Inheriting attributes

8. Which concept allows you to create specialized classes based on existing ones in OOP?

a) Polymorphism

b) Inheritance

c) Encapsulation

d) Abstraction

9. In OOP, what is the purpose of a constructor?

a) To create objects

b) To encapsulate data

c) To override methods

d) To initialize object attributes

10. What is the significance of using abstraction in OOP?
    a) It promotes code reuse
    b) It simplifies complex systems by modeling essential attributes and behaviors
    c) It allows objects to be treated as instances of the same superclass
    d) It bundles data and methods within a class

Answer Key

1. c) Model real-world entities and interactions
2. c) A blueprint that defines the structure and behavior of an object
3. c) An instance of a class, containing attributes and methods
4. a) Inheritance
5. c) The ability of different objects to be treated as instances of the same superclass
6. b) Bundling data and methods within a class
7. b) Hiding implementation details
8. b) Inheritance
9. a) To initialize object attributes
10. b) It simplifies complex systems by modeling essential attributes and behaviors

Short Answer Questions

1. Explain the concept of inheritance in Object-Oriented Programming.
2. What is polymorphism, and how does it contribute to code flexibility in OOP?
3. Describe the process of encapsulation in OOP and its benefits.
4. How does abstraction simplify the design of complex systems in OOP?
5. Provide an example of a real-world scenario where classes and objects could be used to model entities and interactions.
6. Briefly explain the purpose of a constructor in a class.
7. How can you achieve polymorphism through method overriding in Python?
8. Describe the role of attributes and methods in an OOP class.
9. What is the primary advantage of using inheritance in OOP?
10. Why is encapsulation considered a fundamental principle of OOP design?

REGULAR EXPRESSIONS

Introduction to Regular Expressions

Regular expressions are powerful tools for pattern matching and manipulation of strings. They provide a concise and flexible way to search, match, and extract specific patterns of characters in text data. Whether you need to validate user input, extract information from a large dataset, or perform complex text processing tasks, regular expressions are an essential tool in a programmer's toolkit.

At its core, a regular expression is a sequence of characters that defines a search pattern. This pattern can be simple, such as finding a specific word in a sentence, or complex, involving intricate combinations of characters and conditions. Regular expressions allow you to express patterns using metacharacters, quantifiers, character classes, and other syntax elements, providing a compact and expressive language for specifying string patterns.

In the world of programming, regular expressions find applications in various domains. They are extensively used in web development for validating and sanitizing user input, parsing HTML and XML documents, and extracting data from web pages. In data analysis and manipulation, regular expressions help in extracting and transforming textual data, performing data cleaning tasks, and pattern-based data searching. Additionally, regular expressions are commonly employed in system administration tasks, logfile analysis, and text processing in command-line environments.

Python, a popular programming language known for its simplicity and versatility, provides built-in support for regular expressions through the 're' module. This module offers functions and methods that allow you to work with regular expressions in Python programs seamlessly. By leveraging the power of regular expressions in Python, you can perform sophisticated string operations with ease and efficiency.

In this chapter, we will explore the fundamentals of regular expressions and their applications in Python. We will learn how to import and utilize the 're' module and delve into the various functions it provides for regex operations. We will also study the syntax and patterns used in regular expressions, equipping you with the knowledge to create powerful and effective regex patterns.

By mastering regular expressions, you will gain the ability to handle complex text processing tasks efficiently and unlock new possibilities in your programming endeavors. So, let's dive into the world of regular expressions and discover the incredible capabilities they offer!

10.1 Metacharacters

Metacharacters are special characters in regular expressions that carry a predefined meaning. They allow you to specify certain types of characters, positions, or conditions within a pattern. Understanding and utilizing metacharacters is crucial for crafting precise and powerful regular expressions.

Here are some commonly used metacharacters:
- **. (dot):** Matches any single character except a newline. For example, the pattern **a.b** matches strings like "axb", "aab", or "a1b".
- **^ (caret):** Matches the beginning of a string. For example, the pattern **^abc** matches strings that start with "abc", such as "abc123" or "abcdef".
- **$ (dollar):** Matches the end of a string. For example, the pattern **xyz $** matches strings that end with "xyz", such as "123xyz" or "abcxyz".
- *** (asterisk):** Matches zero or more occurrences of the preceding pattern. For example, the pattern **ab*c** matches strings like "ac", "abc", "abbc", or "abbbc".
- **+ (plus):** Matches one or more occurrences of the preceding pattern. For example, the pattern **ab+c** matches strings like "abc", "abbc", or "abbbc", but not "ac".
- **? (question mark):** Matches zero or one occurrence of the preceding pattern. For example, the pattern **ab?c** matches strings like "ac" or "abc", but not "abbc".
- **{} (curly braces):** Matches a specific number of occurrences of the preceding pattern. For example, the pattern **a{3}b** matches strings like "aaab", but not "ab" or "aab".
- **[] (square brackets):** Matches any single character within the brackets. For example, the pattern **[aeiou]** matches any vowel, and **[0-9]** matches any digit.

- **\ (backslash):** Escapes metacharacters or introduces special sequences. For example, the pattern **\d** matches any digit, and **\s** matches any whitespace character.
- **| (pipe):** Matches either the pattern on the left or the pattern on the right. For example, the pattern **cat|dog** matches either "cat" or "dog".

10.2 Using Regular Expressions in Python

Python provides built-in support for regular expressions through the **re** module. This module offers functions and methods to work with regular expressions in Python programs. We will learn how to import and utilize the **re** module to perform various regex operations.

10.2.1 Example: Matching Email Addresses

Let's start with a simple example of matching email addresses using regular expressions in Python:

```
import re
pattern = r"\b[A-Za-z0-9._%+-]+@[A-Za-z0-9.-]+\.[A-Za-z]{2,}\b"
text = "Contact us at info@example.com or support@example.org"
matches = re.findall(pattern, text)
print(matches)
Output:
['info@example.com', 'support@example.org']
```

In this example, we import the re module and define a regular expression pattern to match email addresses. We then apply the findall() function to find all matches of the pattern in the given text. The resulting matches are printed as the output.

10.2.2 Example: Splitting a Text into Words

Regular expressions can also be used to split a text into words based on certain delimiters. Here's an example:

```
import re
pattern = r"\W+" # Matches one or more non-alphanumeric characters
text = "Hello, World! How are you today?"
words = re.split(pattern, text)
print(words)
```

```
Output:
['Hello', 'World', 'How', 'are', 'you', 'today']
```

In this example, we use the split() function from the re module to split the given text into words. The regular expression pattern \W+ matches one or more non-alphanumeric characters, which are used as delimiters to split the text.

These examples demonstrate how to import and use the re module in Python for regular expression operations, including pattern matching and text splitting. Regular expressions provide powerful capabilities for manipulating and analyzing textual data in Python programs.

10.3 Regular Expression Functions

The re module in Python provides several functions for working with regular expressions. We will discuss and demonstrate the usage of important functions such as re.search(), re.match(), re.findall(), and re.sub(). These functions allow us to search for patterns, match patterns at the beginning of strings, find all occurrences of a pattern, and perform pattern substitution, respectively.

10.3.1 Example: Searching for a Pattern

The re.search() function searches for the first occurrence of a pattern in a given string. Here's an example:

```
import re
pattern = r"world"
text = "Hello, World! How are you today?"
match = re.search(pattern, text)
if match:
print("Pattern found:", match.group())
else:
print("Pattern not found.")
Output:
Pattern found: World
```

In this example, we use the re.search() function to search for the pattern "world" in the given text. If a match is found, we print the matched substring using the group() method of the Match object. If no match is found, we print a message indicating that the pattern was not found.

10.3.2 Example: Matching at the Beginning of a String

The re.match() function checks if a pattern matches at the beginning of a string. Here's an example:

```
import re
pattern = r"^Hello"
text = "Hello, World! How are you today?"
match = re.match(pattern, text)
if match:
print("Pattern found:", match.group())
else:
print("Pattern not found.")
Output:
Pattern found: Hello
```

In this example, we use the re.match() function to match the pattern "Hello" at the beginning of the given text. If a match is found, we print the matched substring using the group() method. If no match is found, we print a message indicating that the pattern was not found.

10.3.3 Example: Finding All Occurrences of a Pattern

The re.findall() function finds all non-overlapping occurrences of a pattern in a string. Here's an example:

```
import re
pattern = r"\b\w{4}\b"
text = "Hello, World! How are you today?"
matches = re.findall(pattern, text)
print("Occurrences found:", matches)
Output:
Occurrences found: ['Hello', 'World', 'today']
```

In this example, we use the re.findall() function to find all occurrences of a pattern consisting of exactly four word characters (letters, digits, or underscores) in the given text. The function returns a list of all matched substrings.

10.3.4 Example: Pattern Substitution

The re.sub() function performs pattern substitution in a string. Here's an example:

```
import re
pattern = r"World"
replacement = "Universe"
text = "Hello, World! How are you today?"
new_text = re.sub(pattern, replacement, text)
print("Modified text:", new_text)
```

In this example, we use the re.sub() function to replace all occurrences of the pattern "World" with the replacement string "Universe" in the given text. The function returns a new string with the substitutions applied.

These examples demonstrate the usage of important regular expression functions in Python. The re.search(), re.match(), re.findall(), and re.sub() functions provide powerful capabilities for pattern searching, matching, and substitution in Python programs.

10.4   Regular Expression Patterns

Regular expressions use special characters and syntax to define patterns. We will explore the common metacharacters, quantifiers, character classes, and other elements that form the building blocks of regular expression patterns. Understanding these patterns will enable us to create powerful and expressive regex patterns to match specific strings.

Summary

Regular expressions are a valuable tool for manipulating and searching for patterns in text data. Python's re module provides a convenient way to work with regular expressions, allowing us to perform various operations such as searching, matching, and substitution.

By using regular expressions, you can:
- Search for specific patterns within strings, making it easier to extract relevant information from large amounts of text data.
- Validate and enforce patterns in user input, ensuring that it meets specific criteria or formatting requirements.
- Perform advanced text processing and manipulation tasks, such as replacing, splitting, or rearranging text based on specific patterns.

- Efficiently parse structured data, such as log files or CSV files, by leveraging regular expression patterns to extract relevant fields.
- Regular expressions offer a concise and powerful way to express complex patterns, enabling you to perform precise pattern matching and manipulation. However, they can also be challenging to master, especially for complex scenarios with intricate patterns.

To become proficient in working with regular expressions, it is essential to practice and gain familiarity with the different metacharacters, quantifiers, and character classes. Regular expressions require careful attention to detail and testing to ensure the desired patterns are correctly defined and matched.

By mastering regular expressions, you can enhance your string manipulation capabilities and tackle complex text processing tasks effectively. Regular expressions are widely used in various domains, including data analysis, web development, and system administration, making them a valuable skill for any Python programmer.

Multiple-Choice Questions (MCQs):

1. What is the primary purpose of regular expressions?
   a) Solving mathematical equations
   b) Pattern matching and manipulation of strings
   c) Generating random numbers
   d) Creating graphical user interfaces
2. Which metacharacter matches any single character except a newline?
   a) ?
   b) ^
   c) .
   d) +
3. Which regular expression function is used to search for the first occurrence of a pattern in a string?
   a) re.match()
   b) re.find()
   c) re.search()
   d) re.match_first()

4. The pattern "\d{3}-\d{2}-\d{4}" is used to match what kind of data?
   a) Email addresses
   b) Phone numbers in a specific format
   c) URLs
   d) Social security numbers

5. Which metacharacter is used to match the end of a string?
   a) $
   b) %
   c) &
   d) *

6. What does the re.findall() function return?
   a) The index of the first match
   b) The count of matches found
   c) A list of all matched substrings
   d) The matched substring

7. Which regular expression pattern matches any vowel?
   a) [a-z]
   b) [0-9]
   c) [A-Za-z]
   d) [aeiou]

8. The re.split() function is used for:
   a) Combining strings
   b) Converting strings to lowercase
   c) Splitting a string based on a pattern
   d) Reversing a string

9. Which metacharacter is used to match one or more occurrences of the preceding pattern?
   a) *
   b) +
   c) ?
   d) {

10. What is the purpose of using the re.sub() function?
    a) Searching for a pattern in a string
    b) Extracting all occurrences of a pattern
    c) Splitting a string into words
    d) Replacing occurrences of a pattern with a replacement string

Answer Key:

1. b) Pattern matching and manipulation of strings
2. c).
3. c) re.search()
4. b) Phone numbers in a specific format
5. $
6. A list of all matched substrings
7. [aeiou]
8. Splitting a string based on a pattern
9. b) +
10. Replacing occurrences of a pattern with a replacement string

Short Answer Questions:

1. Define regular expressions and explain their significance in text processing.
2. List and briefly explain three applications of regular expressions in programming.
3. Explain the role of metacharacters in defining regular expression patterns.
4. Provide an example of a regular expression that matches email addresses.
5. Describe the purpose of the **re.search()** function and provide an example of its usage.
6. How does the **re.match()** function differ from the **re.search()** function? Give an example.
7. Explain the usage of the **re.findall()** function with an example.
8. Describe the concept of quantifiers in regular expressions and give an example of a quantifier.
9. How can the **re.split()** function be used to split a text into words? Provide an example.
10. What is the purpose of the **re.sub()** function? Provide an example of replacing a pattern in a string.

DEBUGGING AND TESTING IN PYTHON 11

Introduction

In the world of software development, creating a functional and reliable program is a complex task that often involves navigating through various challenges. Two critical components that contribute to the success of any software project are debugging and testing. Debugging is the process of identifying and rectifying errors or "bugs" in your code, ensuring that it operates as intended. Testing, on the other hand, is the systematic evaluation of your code to confirm its correctness and reliability across different scenarios.

Debugging is akin to a detective's work in the programming world. As programmers, we craft intricate code structures, and as with any complex task, there's always room for errors. These errors can range from syntax mistakes, logic flaws, to unexpected behavior under specific conditions. Debugging is the systematic process of tracking down these issues and rectifying them to ensure the program operates smoothly.

The importance of effective debugging cannot be overstated. Detecting and fixing errors early in the development process saves time, minimizes frustration, and ultimately leads to the creation of more robust and reliable software. Debugging also aids in identifying the root causes of issues, which often leads to an improved understanding of the program's inner workings.

Testing, on the other hand, is a broader practice that ensures the overall quality and reliability of your software. It involves examining your code systematically to verify that it functions as expected across various scenarios and inputs. Through testing, you not only validate the correctness of your code but also confirm that it behaves predictably and consistently.

Testing is essential because it helps catch errors that might not be immediately apparent during the development phase. It enables you to identify issues that could arise when your program interacts with real-world data or user input. Furthermore, comprehensive testing instills confidence in your code and helps prevent potential setbacks when your software is deployed to users.

In this chapter, we embark on a journey through the realms of debugging and testing in Python. We will delve into a variety of techniques, strategies, and tools that empower programmers to identify and rectify issues in their code while ensuring its correctness. From mastering the art of strategically placed print statements to utilizing specialized debugging tools, we will explore methods to track the flow of program execution and examine the values of variables.

We will also dive into various testing strategies, such as unit testing, integration testing, and functional testing. These approaches enable you to methodically evaluate different facets of your software, from individual components to the interactions between them. Additionally, we will discuss concepts like test-driven development (TDD), where writing tests before code can lead to more maintainable and dependable software.

Ultimately, the goal of this chapter is to equip you with the knowledge and tools needed to navigate the intricacies of debugging and testing in Python. By embracing these practices, you can elevate the quality of your programs, enhance user satisfaction, and contribute to a more resilient software ecosystem. So, let's embark on this enlightening journey and unravel the world of debugging and testing in Python.

11.1   Debugging Techniques

When it comes to programming, encountering bugs and errors is a common occurrence. Debugging, the process of identifying and resolving these issues, is an essential skill for every developer. Effective debugging not only ensures the functionality of your code but also enhances your problem-solving capabilities. In this section, we will explore various debugging techniques that can empower you to tackle issues in your Python programs with confidence.

11.1.1   Print Statements: A Simple yet Powerful Approach

One of the simplest and most accessible debugging techniques is the strategic placement of print statements within your code. By inserting print statements at crucial points in your program, you can gain insights into the flow of execution and the values of variables at specific moments.

Print statements serve as breadcrumbs that guide you through the program's journey. You can use them to track the order in which certain functions are executed, observe the values of variables before and after particular operations, and identify potential bottlenecks in your code.

For instance, if you're encountering unexpected behavior in a loop, you can place print statements inside the loop to observe the iteration process and the values of loop variables. This can help you pinpoint the source of the issue and make necessary corrections.

11.1.2 Harnessing Debugging Tools

Python comes equipped with powerful built-in debugging tools, and one of the standout tools is the Python Debugger (pdb) module. pdb enables you to step through your code, set breakpoints, inspect variables, and navigate the program's execution interactively.

Setting breakpoints allows you to pause the execution of your code at specific lines, giving you the opportunity to examine the state of variables and the flow of execution up to that point. You can then proceed step by step through the code, observing how variables change and identifying any discrepancies.

The pdb module is particularly valuable when dealing with complex programs or scenarios where print statements might not provide sufficient insights. It provides a more granular and interactive approach to debugging, enabling you to get closer to the root causes of errors.

11.1.3 Logging: Recording Insights for Analysis

While print statements are effective for immediate insights during development, logging offers a more organized and structured approach to tracking program execution. The logging module in Python provides the means to record valuable information about your program's behavior and performance in log files.

By strategically placing logging messages at different levels of severity (debug, info, warning, error, etc.), you can create a detailed record of how your program behaves. Logging is especially useful when you need to monitor a program in production environments or identify issues that might not manifest during development.

Furthermore, logging allows you to toggle the level of detail you want to capture. During development, you might opt for verbose logging to thoroughly examine the program's execution. In production, you can dial down the logging to capture only critical information.

11.1.4 Assertions: Validating Assumptions

Assertions are powerful tools that assist in validating assumptions about your code. An assertion is a statement that tests whether a given condition holds true. If the condition is false, an assertion error is raised, halting the program's execution and providing you with valuable information about the encountered issue.

Using assertions, you can express your expectations about the values of variables, the state of objects, or the outcome of specific operations. If any of these expectations are not met, the assertion error serves as an early warning system, highlighting potential problems.

Assertions can be particularly useful when dealing with complex code paths or when making assumptions about the correctness of inputs. By systematically verifying these assumptions, you can catch errors at an early stage and prevent them from propagating to later parts of your program.

11.2 Testing Strategies

As a software developer, ensuring that your code performs as expected and produces reliable results is of utmost importance. This is where testing comes into play. A well-thought-out testing strategy enables you to systematically evaluate your code's behavior, catch errors, and ensure that your software functions smoothly across various scenarios. In this section, we'll explore different testing strategies that play a vital role in guaranteeing the quality and correctness of your Python programs.

11.2.1 Unit Testing: The Building Blocks of Quality

Unit testing involves breaking down your code into smaller, manageable components—units—and testing each unit in isolation. The goal is to ascertain that each individual component functions as expected before integrating them into the larger program. Python's unittest framework provides a structured approach to creating and executing unit tests.

By writing unit tests, you can validate the behavior of functions, methods, or classes under different inputs and conditions. Each unit test should cover specific scenarios, such as edge cases and typical use cases. A comprehensive suite of unit tests serves as a safety net that helps detect issues early in the development process, making debugging more efficient and reliable.

11.2.2 Integration Testing: Ensuring Seamless Collaboration

While unit testing focuses on individual components, integration testing shifts the spotlight to the interactions between different components of your code. This strategy ensures that units work together seamlessly and that the program as a whole functions correctly.

Integration testing is vital for catching issues that may arise when components interact. It verifies that data flows smoothly between units and that they cooperate as expected. These tests uncover issues like incompatible interfaces, communication breakdowns, and other integration-related problems that can't be identified through unit testing alone.

11.2.3 Functional Testing: Verifying Program Functionality

Functional testing takes a broader perspective by examining the functionality of your entire program. It involves testing various scenarios, user interactions, and input combinations to ensure that your software meets its specified requirements and delivers the intended outcomes.

Functional testing encompasses a wide range of scenarios, from basic use cases to complex user interactions. It verifies that your program behaves as expected under different conditions and doesn't exhibit unexpected behavior. This strategy helps uncover logic errors, functional discrepancies, and issues that may emerge due to unforeseen user actions.

11.2.4 Regression Testing: Safeguarding Against Regressions

Regression testing ensures that new code changes do not inadvertently introduce new bugs or cause existing functionality to break. As your codebase evolves, new features are added, and existing code is modified. Regression testing ensures that these changes don't compromise the stability and reliability of your software.

Automated regression testing is particularly valuable. Automated tests can be run consistently and frequently to validate that existing functionality remains intact with each code update. By automating these tests, you can quickly identify and address regressions, maintaining code quality over time.

A comprehensive testing strategy is a cornerstone of software development, enhancing the quality, reliability, and maintainability of your Python programs. Unit testing, integration testing, functional testing, and regression testing collectively provide a safety net that catches errors early, prevents unexpected behavior, and promotes continuous improvement. By incorporating these testing strategies into your development process, you can confidently produce software that not only meets expectations but also withstands the challenges of the ever-evolving software landscape.

11.3   Test-Driven Development (TDD)

Test-Driven Development (TDD) is more than just a testing technique; it's a holistic development approach that revolves around writing tests before writing the actual code. TDD introduces a structured and iterative cycle that encourages thoughtful design, precise implementation, and continuous refinement of your codebase. In this section, we'll dive into the principles and benefits of Test-Driven Development and explore how it can revolutionize your approach to software development in Python.

The TDD Cycle: Write, Test, Refactor

TDD operates on a simple yet powerful cycle: write a failing test, write the minimum code to make the test pass, and then refactor the code to improve its design and maintainability. This cycle guides you through the development process while ensuring that every piece of functionality is thoroughly tested and validated.

1. Write a Failing Test: The TDD cycle begins by identifying a specific piece of functionality you want to implement. You start by writing a test that captures the desired behavior. Since you haven't written any code yet, this test is expected to fail initially.

2. Write the Minimum Code: With a failing test in place, your goal is to write the minimum amount of code necessary to make the test pass. This often involves implementing the required functionality in a straightforward manner.

3. Refactor for Better Design: Once your test passes, you enter the refactoring phase. This is where you can improve the design, structure, and readability of your code without changing its behavior. The refactoring process ensures that your code remains clean and maintainable.

Benefits of TDD

Test-Driven Development offers a range of benefits that contribute to the overall quality and reliability of your codebase:

- Improved Code Quality: TDD encourages thoughtful planning and design before writing code. This results in more structured and organized code that is easier to understand and maintain.
- Early Bug Detection: By writing tests first, you identify issues and bugs early in the development process. This enables you to catch and fix problems before they propagate through the codebase.
- Confidence in Refactoring: Refactoring is a crucial aspect of software development. With a suite of tests in place, you can confidently make changes to your codebase, knowing that tests will promptly catch any unintended side effects.
- Living Documentation: Tests serve as living documentation that describes the intended behavior of your code. They provide insight into how different components should interact and respond to various inputs.
- Regulation of Feature Creep: TDD encourages you to focus on writing code only to fulfill specific test cases. This prevents unnecessary features from being added, leading to more focused and streamlined software.

Adopting TDD in Python

To embrace TDD in Python, start by identifying the smallest piece of functionality you want to implement. Write a test that defines the expected behavior of that functionality. As you implement the necessary code to make the test pass, remember that your initial implementation doesn't need to be perfect. Refactor the code to improve its design, and ensure that your test continues to pass.

Python provides testing frameworks like unittest and third-party libraries like pytest that facilitate the TDD process. These tools enable you to organize your tests, run them automatically, and generate meaningful test reports.

Test-Driven Development is a transformative approach that emphasizes the importance of testing, design, and iteration. By writing tests before code, you cultivate a habit of focused development and ensure that your software meets the desired specifications. TDD not only enhances code quality and reliability but also promotes collaboration and empowers you to adapt to changing requirements with confidence. Integrating TDD into your development workflow can lead to more resilient, maintainable, and well-structured Python programs.

11.4   Continuous Integration (CI) and Continuous Deployment (CD)

In the fast-paced world of software development, ensuring code quality, reliability, and timely deployment is paramount. Continuous Integration (CI) and Continuous Deployment (CD) are practices that address these challenges by automating key aspects of the development and deployment process. These practices not only streamline development workflows but also contribute to the creation of robust and dependable software. In this section, we'll delve into the concepts of CI and CD, explore their benefits, and understand how they can revolutionize your Python development process.

11.4.1   Continuous Integration (CI): Ensuring Code Quality

Continuous Integration (CI) revolves around the practice of automatically integrating code changes into a shared repository multiple times a day. With CI, developers frequently commit their code changes, triggering automated tests that validate the integrity of the codebase. This process ensures that new code changes do not introduce regressions or conflicts with existing functionality.

The CI Workflow:
1.   Developers work on their respective code changes in feature branches.
2.   When a developer completes their changes, they create a pull request to merge their code into the main repository.
3.   Automated tests, including unit tests and integration tests, are run on the pull request to verify its correctness.
4.   If the tests pass, the pull request is merged into the main repository.
5.   The CI system deploys the updated code to a testing environment, allowing for further validation.

CI emphasizes the importance of rapid feedback loops. If a test fails or a conflict arises, developers are notified immediately, enabling them to address the issues promptly. This practice leads to early bug detection, encourages a collaborative development process, and maintains code quality throughout the project's lifecycle.

11.4.2   Continuous Deployment (CD): Automating Deployment

Continuous Deployment (CD) takes the principles of CI a step further by automating the deployment of code changes to production environments. With CD, validated code changes are automatically deployed to production servers, minimizing manual intervention and reducing the risk of human errors during deployment.

The CD Workflow:

1. Code changes pass all automated tests in the CI environment.
2. The validated code changes are automatically deployed to a staging or production environment.
3. Automated tests specific to deployment, such as smoke tests and end-to-end tests, are executed to ensure that the deployment was successful.
4. If the deployment passes all tests, the changes are made live in the production environment.

CD not only accelerates the release process but also increases the reliability of deployments. By minimizing the manual steps involved, CD reduces the likelihood of deployment errors and inconsistencies between environments. This practice enables teams to deliver features and updates to users faster, promoting a consistent and iterative development process.

Adopting CI/CD in Python Development

To embrace CI/CD in Python development, you can utilize various tools and services that support these practices. Version control systems like Git provide the foundation for CI/CD workflows, enabling developers to collaborate on code changes. CI/CD platforms like Jenkins, Travis CI, CircleCI, and GitHub Actions offer automated testing and deployment capabilities.

By integrating CI/CD into your Python development workflow, you create a pipeline that ensures code quality, rapid feedback, and reliable deployment. This approach fosters a culture of continuous improvement and empowers your team to deliver software with confidence.

Continuous Integration (CI) and Continuous Deployment (CD) practices provide the foundation for efficient, reliable, and rapid software development. By automating testing and deployment processes, CI/CD enhances collaboration, accelerates feedback loops, and reduces the risks associated with manual interventions. By integrating these practices into your

Python development, you can create a streamlined, iterative, and dependable software development lifecycle that adapts to changing requirements and delivers high-quality solutions to users.

Summary

- Debugging and testing are essential in software development.
- Debugging identifies and fixes errors, while testing verifies correctness.
- Debugging is like a detective's work, addressing syntax, logic, and behavior issues.
- Effective debugging saves time, enhances understanding, and leads to robust software.
- Testing confirms correct behavior, catches errors, and builds user confidence.
- Debugging is crucial for identifying and resolving issues in code.
- Print statements offer a simple way to track execution flow and variable values.
- Python Debugger (pdb) allows interactive inspection and breakpoint setting.
- Logging records program execution for analysis, aiding debugging.
- Assertions validate assumptions; assertion errors provide early warnings.
- Unit testing tests individual code components in isolation.
- Integration testing focuses on interactions between code components.
- Functional testing examines overall program functionality under various conditions.
- Regression testing ensures new code doesn't introduce bugs or break existing functionality.
- TDD is a development approach writing tests before code.
- TDD cycle: write a failing test, write code to pass, refactor for design.
- Benefits: improved code quality, early bug detection, confidence in refactoring.
- TDD leads to focused development, clean code, and living documentation.
- CI automates integration of code changes, ensuring correctness and preventing regressions.
- CD automates deployment of validated code changes to production environments.

- CI/CD reduces manual errors, accelerates deployment, and promotes collaboration.
- Use version control systems (e.g., Git) as the foundation.
- CI/CD platforms (Jenkins, Travis CI, GitHub Actions) automate testing and deployment.
- CI/CD practices create a streamlined and dependable development process.

Multiple-Choice Questions (MCQs):'

1. What is the primary goal of debugging in software development?
   a) Writing new code
   b) Identifying and fixing errors
   c) Documenting code
   d) Refactoring code
2. Which of the following is a common debugging technique?
   a) Writing pseudocode
   b) Using magic numbers
   c) Placing print statements
   d) Ignoring errors
3. Which Python module provides an interactive debugger?
   a) debuglib
   b) debugtools
   c) pdb
   d) inspect
4. What is the purpose of assertions in debugging?
   a) To display error messages to users
   b) To validate assumptions about code
   c) To ignore errors in the code
   d) To suppress warnings
5. Which type of testing focuses on testing individual components in isolation?
   a) Regression testing
   b) Integration testing
   c) Unit testing
   d) Functional testing

6. What is the benefit of automated regression testing?
   a) It catches new bugs and errors.
   b) It reduces the need for debugging.
   c) It prevents code changes.
   d) It maintains code quality over time.
7. Which development approach involves writing tests before writing the actual code?
   a) Debug-Driven Development (DDD)
   b) Test-First Development (TFD)
   c) Test-Driven Development (TDD)
   d) Code-Testing Development (CTD)
8. What is the purpose of continuous integration (CI)?
   a) Automating deployment to production
   b) Running tests for every code change
   c) Ignoring code changes
   d) Isolating developers from each other
9. Which practice involves automating the deployment of code changes to production environments?
   a) Continuous Integration (CI)
   b) Continuous Testing (CT)
   c) Continuous Deployment (CD)
   d) Continuous Debugging (CD)
10. Which tool provides automated testing and deployment capabilities for CI/CD?
    a) Git
    b) Python Debugger (pdb)
    c) Jenkins
    d) UnitTest

Answer Key

1. b) Identifying and fixing errors
2. c) Placing print statements
3. c) pdb
4. b) To validate assumptions about code
5. c) Unit testing
6. e) It maintains code quality over time

7. c) Test-Driven Development (TDD)
8. b) Running tests for every code change
9. c) Continuous Deployment (CD)
10. c) Jenkins

Short Answer Questions:

1. What is the purpose of using print statements for debugging? Provide an example.
2. Explain the concept of breakpoints in debugging and how they are useful.
3. Describe the role of the Python Debugger (pdb) module in debugging.
4. How does logging differ from using print statements for debugging purposes?
5. What is the significance of assertions in testing and debugging? Provide an example.
6. Differentiate between unit testing and integration testing in terms of scope and purpose.
7. What is regression testing, and why is it important in software development?
8. Explain the concept of Test-Driven Development (TDD) and its three-step cycle.
9. How does TDD contribute to code quality and early bug detection?
10. Define Continuous Integration (CI) and Continuous Deployment (CD) and explain how they enhance the development process.

ADVANCED TOPICS IN PYTHON PROGRAMMING

12

Introduction

In this chapter, we will take a deeper dive into advanced concepts that elevate your Python programming skills. Building upon the foundation you've developed through previous chapters, we'll explore sophisticated techniques that enable you to write more efficient, flexible, and powerful code.

12.1: Generators

Generators are a fundamental concept in Python that revolutionizes the way we work with sequences, especially when dealing with large datasets or infinite sequences. Unlike traditional functions that compute and return values immediately, generators allow for lazy evaluation, meaning they produce values on-the-fly as needed. This not only conserves memory but also provides efficient ways to handle data that would otherwise be impractical to store in memory all at once.

Understanding the Basics of Generators:

At the core of generators is the yield keyword. When a function contains a yield statement, it becomes a generator function. Instead of returning a value with the return keyword, a generator function yields a value using yield. When the function is called, it doesn't execute the entire code block at once. Instead, it starts executing and pauses at the yield statement, allowing the yielded value to be retrieved.

Example 1: Infinite Sequence Generator

```
def infinite_
onacci():
```

```
a, b = 0, 1
while True:
yield a
a, b = b, a + b
# Create a generator object
fib_generator = infinite_fibonacci()
# Generate Fibonacci numbers on-the-fly
for _ in range(10):
print(next(fib_generator))
```

Example 2: Lazy File Reading

```
def read_large_file(file_path):
with open(file_path, 'r') as file:
for line in file:
yield line
# Create a generator for reading a large file
file_generator = read_large_file('large_data.txt')
# Process lines from the file one by one
for line in file_generator:
process_line(line)
```

Generator Expressions: In addition to defining generator functions, you can also use generator expressions to create generators in a concise manner. These are similar to list comprehensions but generate values lazily, without creating an entire list in memory.

Example 3: Generator Expression

```
squared_numbers = (x ** 2 for x in range(1, 11))
for num in squared_numbers:
print(num)
```

12.1.1   Benefits of Generators:

Memory Efficiency: Generators allow you to work with large datasets without loading everything into memory at once. This is crucial for tasks like processing log files, streaming data, or working with databases.

Infinite Sequences: Generators make it possible to work with sequences that are conceptually infinite, like the Fibonacci sequence. You can iterate over them as needed without worrying about memory limitations.

Efficient Pipelines: Generators can be chained together to create processing pipelines, where data flows through a series of transformations without being fully loaded into memory at any point.

Reduced Computation: Lazy evaluation means that computations are only performed when needed, leading to faster execution in scenarios where not all values are required.

Generators are a cornerstone of Python's ability to handle data efficiently, especially when working with large or dynamic datasets. They provide a flexible and memory-conscious way to process and generate values on-the-fly, enhancing the performance and versatility of your programs.

12.2   Decorators: Transforming Functions with Ease

Decorators are a powerful feature in Python that allow you to modify or enhance the behavior of functions or methods without altering their core code. They enable you to encapsulate reusable functionality and promote clean, modular, and maintainable code. Decorators are especially useful for tasks such as logging, authentication, caching, and performance profiling.

Understanding the Basics of Decorators:

A decorator is a function that takes another function as input and returns a new function that usually extends or modifies the behavior of the original function. Decorators are often used with the @ symbol followed by the decorator function's name, placed above the function definition.

Example 1: Creating a Simple Decorator

```
def uppercase_decorator(func):
def wrapper(*args, **kwargs):
result = func(*args, **kwargs)
return result.upper()
return wrapper
```

```
@uppercase_decorator
def greet(name):
return f"Hello, {name}"
print(greet("Alice")) # Outputs: "HELLO, ALICE"
```

Example 2: Creating a Decorator with Parameters

```
def repeat_decorator(times):
def decorator(func):
def wrapper(*args, **kwargs):
result = ""
for _ in range(times):
result += func(*args, **kwargs)
return result
return wrapper
return decorator
@repeat_decorator(times=3)
def say_hello(name):
return f"Hello, {name}! "
print(say_hello("Bob")) # Outputs: "Hello, Bob! Hello, Bob! Hello, Bob! "
```

Built-in Decorators: Python comes with several built-in decorators that provide convenient and meaningful functionality for methods within classes. Examples include **@staticmethod** and **@classmethod**, which are used to define static and class methods, respectively.

Example 3: Using @staticmethod and @classmethod

```
class MathOperations:
@staticmethod
def add(x, y):
return x + y
@classmethod
def multiply(cls, x, y):
return cls.add(x, y) * 2
print(MathOperations.add(3, 5)) # Outputs: 8
print(MathOperations.multiply(3, 5)) # Outputs: 16
```

Benefits of Decorators:

1. **Modular Code:** Decorators promote modular programming by allowing you to separate concerns and reuse functionality across multiple functions.
2. **Code Reusability:** Instead of repeating the same code across functions, you can encapsulate it in a decorator and apply it wherever needed.
3. **Clean Syntax:** Decorator syntax using @ makes code more readable and concise, especially when dealing with repetitive tasks.
4. **Aspect-Oriented Programming:** Decorators enable the concept of aspect-oriented programming, where cross-cutting concerns are handled separately from the main logic.

Common Use Cases for Decorators:

1. **Logging:** Decorators can log function calls, arguments, and return values for debugging and monitoring purposes.
2. **Caching:** Decorators can cache expensive function calls to improve performance.
3. **Authorization and Authentication:** Decorators can enforce access control by checking user roles or permissions.
4. **Memoization:** Decorators can store the results of expensive function calls to avoid redundant computations.
5. **Validation:** Decorators can validate function inputs before execution.

Decorators provide an elegant and efficient way to enhance the behavior of functions or methods without cluttering their core logic. By leveraging decorators, you can streamline code, promote reusability, and simplify the implementation of common functionalities across your Python projects.

12.3   Context Managers: Simplifying Resource Management

Resource management is a critical aspect of programming, especially when dealing with external resources like files, network connections, or database connections. Properly acquiring and releasing resources is essential to prevent memory leaks and ensure the stability of your applications. Context managers, introduced through the **with** statement in Python, provide an elegant and foolproof way to manage resources by automatically handling their allocation and deallocation.

Understanding Context Managers: A context manager is an object that defines the methods __**enter**__() and __**exit**__() to manage the acquisition and release of resources. When a context manager is used with the **with** statement, it ensures that the resource is acquired before entering the block and released after exiting the block, regardless of whether an exception occurs.

Example 1: Using the with Statement for Files

```python
with open("example.txt", "r") as file:
content = file.read()
# File is automatically closed when exiting the block
print(content)
```

Creating Custom Context Managers: You can create your own context managers by defining classes with __**enter**__() and __**exit**__() methods. Alternatively, you can use the **contextlib** module to create context managers using generator functions.

Example 2: Creating a Custom Context Manager

```python
class Timer:
def __enter__(self):
self.start_time = time.time()
return self
def __exit__(self, exc_type, exc_value, exc_traceback):
self.end_time = time.time()
self.elapsed_time = self.end_time - self.start_time
print(f"Elapsed time: {self.elapsed_time} seconds")
with Timer():
time.sleep(2)
# Output: Elapsed time: 2.000020742416382 seconds
```

Example 3: Using contextlib to Create a Context Manager

```python
from contextlib import contextmanager
@contextmanager
def custom_open(file_name, mode):
```

```
file = open(file_name, mode)
try:
yield file
finally:
file.close()
with custom_open("example.txt", "r") as file:
content = file.read()
```

Benefits of Context Managers:

1. **Automated Resource Management:** Context managers ensure proper acquisition and release of resources, reducing the risk of memory leaks.
2. **Cleaner Code:** Context managers simplify resource management, leading to cleaner and more readable code.
3. **Exception Safety:** Resources are released even if exceptions occur within the **with** block.
4. **Avoiding Repetition:** Context managers eliminate the need to write boilerplate code for resource allocation and deallocation.

Common Use Cases for Context Managers:

1. **File Operations:** Automatically close files after reading or writing.
2. **Database Connections:** Ensure that database connections are properly closed.
3. **Locks and Semaphores:** Manage synchronization primitives for multithreaded applications.
4. **Network Connections:** Automatically close network sockets after use.
5. **Custom Resource Management:** Any situation where resource allocation and deallocation are involved.

By using context managers, you simplify resource management and improve the reliability of your code. With context managers, you can focus on your main logic without worrying about the intricacies of resource acquisition and release. This leads to more robust and maintainable code that is less prone to bugs and memory leaks.

12.4 Metaclasses: Masters of Class Creation

Metaclasses are a powerful and advanced concept in Python that allow you to customize the behavior of class creation. They define the structure and attributes of classes themselves and act as blueprints for the classes that are created using them. While metaclasses might seem complex at first glance, they provide a unique level of control over class behavior and can be used to enforce coding standards, implement design patterns, and much more.

Understanding Metaclasses: In Python, everything is an object, including classes themselves. Just as classes are used to create instances of objects, metaclasses are used to create classes. The concept can be a bit abstract, but let's break it down with an example:

```python
class MyMeta(type):
def __new__(cls, name, bases, attrs):
# Modify attributes before class creation
attrs['additional_attr'] = 42
return super().__new__(cls, name, bases, attrs)
class MyClass(metaclass=MyMeta):
my_class_attr = "Hello, world!"
obj = MyClass()
print(obj.my_class_attr) # Outputs: Hello, world!
print(obj.additional_attr) # Outputs: 42
```

In this example, **MyMeta** is a metaclass that inherits from the built-in **type** class. It overrides the __**new**__() method to modify the attributes of the class before it is created. When **MyClass** is defined with **metaclass=MyMeta**, the __**new**__() method of **MyMeta** is called to customize the class creation process.

Use Cases of Metaclasses: Metaclasses provide a unique level of control over class creation and can be used for various purposes:

- **Code Injection:** You can automatically inject methods, attributes, or behavior into classes as they are defined.
- **Enforcing Coding Standards:** Metaclasses can enforce naming conventions, attribute validation, or other coding standards across classes.
- **Singleton Pattern:** You can use metaclasses to enforce the singleton pattern, ensuring that a class has only one instance.

- **Custom ORM Frameworks:** Metaclasses are commonly used in Object-Relational Mapping (ORM) frameworks to generate database-related code.

While metaclasses are not often needed in everyday programming, they can be extremely powerful when used appropriately. They allow you to shape the structure of your codebase and define class behavior at a higher level, making them a tool for advanced Python developers.

12.5 Multithreading: Managing Concurrent Execution

Multithreading is a technique used to execute multiple threads concurrently within a single process. Python's **threading** module provides a way to create and manage threads, allowing you to take advantage of multiple CPU cores and improve the performance of your applications. However, multithreading also comes with challenges, such as race conditions and synchronization issues.

Creating Threads: The **threading** module in Python makes it relatively easy to create and manage threads. Here's a simple example of how to create and start two threads that perform different tasks concurrently:

```python
import threading
def task1():
for _ in range(5):
print("Task 1 executing")
def task2():
for _ in range(5):
print("Task 2 executing")
thread1 = threading.Thread(target=task1)
thread2 = threading.Thread(target=task2)
thread1.start()
thread2.start()
thread1.join()
thread2.join()
print("All tasks completed")
```

In this example, two threads are created using the **threading.Thread()** class. The **target** parameter specifies the function to be executed by the thread. The **start()** method is used to start the threads, and the **join()** method ensures that the main program waits for the threads to complete before proceeding.

Race Conditions and Synchronization: Race conditions occur when multiple threads access shared resources concurrently, leading to unexpected behavior or incorrect results. Synchronization mechanisms are used to prevent race conditions. One common synchronization primitive is the Lock:

```python
import threading
counter = 0
counter_lock = threading.Lock()
def increment_counter():
global counter
for _ in range(1000000):
with counter_lock:
counter += 1
thread1 = threading.Thread(target=increment_counter)
thread2 = threading.Thread(target=increment_counter)
thread1.start()
thread2.start()
thread1.join()
thread2.join()
print("Counter value:", counter)
```

In this example, two threads increment the **counter** variable by a million times each. The **counter_lock** ensures that only one thread can access and modify the **counter** at a time, preventing race conditions.

GIL Limitation: It's important to note that Python has a Global Interpreter Lock (GIL), which prevents multiple threads from executing Python bytecodes in parallel in a single process. This limitation can impact the performance of CPU-bound tasks in multithreaded Python programs. However, multithreading can still be beneficial for I/O-bound tasks where the threads spend time waiting for external resources.

Mastering Multithreading: While multithreading can provide significant performance improvements, it's essential to carefully manage shared resources and synchronization to avoid race conditions and other issues. With proper understanding and practice, you can write responsive and efficient applications that leverage the full potential of modern hardware.

12.6   GUI Programming with Tkinter: Building User Interfaces

Graphical User Interfaces (GUIs) play a crucial role in modern software applications, providing users with a visual way to interact with programs. Tkinter is Python's standard GUI library, and it offers a simple yet powerful toolkit for creating graphical windows, widgets, and interactive elements.

Creating a Basic Window: Here's a simple example of how to create a basic window using Tkinter:

```python
import tkinter as tk
root = tk.Tk()
root.title("My GUI Application")
root.geometry("300x200")
label = tk.Label(root, text="Hello, Tkinter!")
label.pack()
root.mainloop()
```

In this example, we import the **tkinter** module and create a root window using **tk.Tk()**. We set the window title and dimensions using **title()** and **geometry()** methods. Then, we create a **Label** widget to display text and use the **pack()** method to place it within the window. Finally, we start the GUI event loop with **mainloop()**.

Handling Button Clicks: Interactive elements like buttons are fundamental in GUI applications. Here's an example of how to create a button and handle its click event:

```python
import tkinter as tk
def on_button_click():
label.config(text="Button clicked!")
root = tk.Tk()
root.title("Button Example")
label = tk.Label(root, text="Press the button")
label.pack()
button = tk.Button(root, text="Click me", command=on_button_click)
button.pack()
root.mainloop()
```

In this example, we define a function **on_button_click()** that updates the label's text when the button is clicked. The **Button** widget's **command** parameter is set to the function that should be executed on button click.

Layout Management: Tkinter provides various layout managers to control how widgets are arranged within a window. The **pack()**, **grid()**, and **place()** methods allow you to control widget placement. Here's an example using the **grid()** layout manager:

```python
import tkinter as tk
root = tk.Tk()
root.title("Grid Layout Example")
label1 = tk.Label(root, text="Label 1")
label2 = tk.Label(root, text="Label 2")
label3 = tk.Label(root, text="Label 3")
label1.grid(row=0, column=0)
label2.grid(row=0, column=1)
label3.grid(row=1, column=0, columnspan=2)
root.mainloop()
```

In this example, we use the **grid()** layout manager to arrange labels in a grid. The **row** and **column** parameters determine the position of each label, and **columnspan** allows a widget to span multiple columns.

With Tkinter, you can create a wide range of graphical interfaces for your Python applications. By understanding how to create windows, widgets, and handle events, you'll be able to design user-friendly applications that provide a seamless and engaging experience. Tkinter's simplicity and versatility make it an excellent choice for beginners and experienced developers alike.

12.7 Web Development with Flask: Building Web Applications

Web development has become an integral part of software engineering, and Flask is a popular Python web framework that simplifies the process of building web applications. Let's explore the basics of web development using Flask, including defining routes, handling requests and responses, and integrating templates for dynamic content generation.

Setting Up Flask: Before we delve into examples, make sure you have Flask installed. You can install it using pip:

```
pip install Flask
```

Creating a Basic Web Application: Here's a simple example of how to create a basic Flask web application:

```python
from flask import Flask
app = Flask(__name__)
@app.route('/')
def hello():
return 'Hello, Flask!'
if __name__ == '__main__':
app.run()
```

In this example, we import the **Flask** class from the **flask** module. We create an instance of the **Flask** class and define a route using the **@app.route()** decorator. The **hello()** function is associated with the root URL ("/"), and it returns the "Hello, Flask!" message.

Handling Dynamic Routes: Flask allows you to create dynamic routes that capture variable values from the URL. Here's an example:

```python
from flask import Flask
app = Flask(__name__)
@app.route('/user/<username>')
def show_user_profile(username):
return f'User: {username}'
if __name__ == '__main__':
app.run()
```

In this example, the show_user_profile() function takes a username parameter from the URL and displays it in the response.

Using Templates for Dynamic Content: Flask integrates with Jinja2 templates for rendering dynamic content. Here's an example of rendering a template with dynamic data:

1. Create a directory named "templates" in your project directory.
2. Inside the "templates" directory, create a file named "hello.html" with the following content:

```
<!doctype html>
<title>Hello, {{ name }}</title>
<h1>Hello, {{ name }}</h1>
```

Now, modify the Flask application to render the template:

```
from flask import Flask, render_template
app = Flask(__name__)
@app.route('/hello/<name>')
def hello(name):
return render_template('hello.html', name=name)
if __name__ == '__main__':
app.run()
```

In this example, the **render_template()** function is used to render the "hello. html" template and pass the **name** variable to it.

Working with Databases: Flask integrates well with various database systems. Here's an example of using SQLite with Flask:

```
from flask import Flask, render_template
from flask_sqlalchemy import SQLAlchemy
app = Flask(__name__)
app.config['SQLALCHEMY_DATABASE_URI'] = 'sqlite:///mydb.db'
db = SQLAlchemy(app)
class User(db.Model):
id = db.Column(db.Integer, primary_key=True)
username = db.Column(db.String(80), unique=True, nullable=False)
@app.route('/users')
def list_users():
users = User.query.all()
return render_template('users.html', users=users)
if __name__ == '__main__':
app.run()
```

In this example, we define a **User** model using SQLAlchemy, which is a popular Object-Relational Mapping (ORM) library. We query the users from the database and render them using a template named "users.html".

Flask provides a solid foundation for web development in Python. By understanding the basics of defining routes, handling requests and responses, integrating templates, and working with databases, you'll be well-equipped to build dynamic and feature-rich web applications. Flask's simplicity and flexibility make it an excellent choice for both beginners and experienced developers entering the world of web development.

Summary

- Lazy evaluation for large datasets or infinite sequences.
- Utilizes yield keyword to produce values on-the-fly.
- yield pauses function, yielding values and conserving memory.
- Generator expressions provide concise creation of generators.
- Modify function behavior without altering core code.
- Created with functions that take and return functions.
- Enhance code with logging, authentication, caching, etc.
- Built-in decorators like @staticmethod and @classmethod.
- Simplify resource management with the with statement.
- Manage resources' allocation and deallocation automatically.
- Custom classes or contextlib for context managers.
- Enhance code robustness, especially with external resources.
- Customize class creation behavior and attributes.
- Blueprint for classes, define with type class.
- Enforce coding standards, implement design patterns.
- Advanced control over class behavior and structure.
- Manage concurrent execution with threads.
- Python's threading module for thread creation.
- Threads utilize multiple CPU cores for performance.
- Handle synchronization and prevent race conditions.
- Tkinter for creating GUIs with windows, widgets, buttons.
- Layout management organizes widget placement.
- Enhance user experience, create interactive applications.
- Flask simplifies web app development in Python.
- Define routes, handle requests and responses.
- Templates for dynamic content using Jinja2.
- Integration with databases for data-driven apps.

ANNEXURE

LIST IN PYTHON

Creating List: A list is created by placing the items/ elements separated by a comma (,) between the square brackets ([]).

```
In []: l1=[1,2,3,56,2.0,'A']
       l1
```

```
Out[]: [1, 2, 3, 56, 2.0, 'A']
```

```
In []: empty_List = []
       integer_List = [26, 12, 97, 8]
       float_List = [5.8, 12.0, 9.7, 10.8]
       string_List = ["Interviewbit", "Preparation", "India"]
       List = [1, "Interviewbit", 9.5, 'D']
       duplicate_List = [1, 2, 1, 1, 3,3, 5, 8, 8]
       print(empty_List) print(integer_List) print(float_List)
       print(string_List)
       print(List) print(duplicate_List)
```

```
[]
[26, 12, 97, 8]
[5.8, 12.0, 9.7, 10.8]
['Interviewbit', 'Preparation', 'India'] [1, 'Interviewbit',
9.5, 'D']
[1, 2, 1, 1, 3, 3, 5, 8, 8]
```

Nested List: Nested list place the various lists separated by comma (,) within the square brackets ([]).

```
In []: nested_List = [[6, 2, 8], [1, "Interviewbit", 3.5], "preparation"]
In []: l1=[1,3,5,2.0]
       l1[2]=12
       l1
```

```
Out[]: [1, 3, 12, 2.0]
```

Indexing: Elements stored in the lists are associated with a unique integer number known as an index. The first element is indexed as 0, and the second is 1, and so on.

We can also access elements/values from the list in python is using a negative index. The negative index starts at -1 for the last element, -2 for the last second element, and so on.

```
In []:      l=[2,40,8,5]
       print(l[1])
       print(l[-1])


       40
       5
```

```
In []:  My_List = [3, 4, 6, 10, 8]
        print("Values accessed using positive Index.") print(My_List[2])
        print(My_List[4])
        print("Values accessed using negative Index.") print(My_List[-1])
        print(My_List[-5])
```

```
Values accessed using positive Index. 6
8
Values accessed using negative Index. 8
3
Nested List Indexing: For nested list we first access the index at
which the inner list is stored/indexed in the outer list using the
index operator. Then we access the element from the inner list using
the index operator again. It is known as nested indexing. It is like
we access elements in a 2-dimensional array.
```

```
In []:  # Nested List
        nested_List = [[6, 2, 8], [1, 3.5, "Interviewbit"],
        "preparation"] print(nested_List[0][1])
        print(nested_List[1][2]) print(nested_List[2])
```

```
2
Interviewbit preparation
Updating List Lists is mutable: i.e Existing values stored at the
indexes can be changed.
```

```
In []:  My_List = [3, 4, 6, 10, 8, 5]
        print(My_List)
        # Changing value to index 3.
        My_List[3] = 7 print(My_List)
        # Changing value to index -1, i.e the last value.
```

```
My_List[-1] = 15 print(My_List)
```

```
[3, 4, 6, 10, 8, 5]
[3, 4, 6, 7, 8, 5]
[3, 4, 6, 7, 8, 15]
Methods in List:
Ex.
My_List=[1,8,7,2]
My_List.append(8) Adds an element at the end of the list.
My_List=[1,8,7,2,8]
My_List.extend(['X',5,'Z']) Adds all elements of one list to another
list. \ My_List=
[1,8,7,2,'X',5,'Z']
My_List.insert(2,'a') Inserts an item at a desired index.
My_List=[1,8,'a',7,2]
My_List.remove(7) Removes an item from the list.
My_List=[1,8,2]
My_List.pop(1) Removes and returns an element at a desired index
My_List=[1,7,2]
```

In []:
```
list1.append(34)
list1.append(2.0)
list1.append('A')
print(list1)
list1.extend([2,3])
print(list1)
list1.insert(2,13)
print(list1)
list1.remove(13)
print(list1)
list1.pop(1)
```

```
[2, 34, 2.0, 'A']
[2, 34, 2.0, 'A', 2, 3]
[2, 34, 13, 2.0, 'A', 2, 3]
[2, 34, 2.0, 'A', 2, 3]
34
```

Out[]:

In []:
```
Lt=[2, 3, 1, 4, 5]
Lt[3] = Lt[1]
[3]
```

Out[]: 3

Methods:

Eg. L2=['A','B',8,5,8]

L2.clear() Removes all elements from the list. output-> L2=[]

L2.index(8) Returns the index of the first identical item. output-> 2

L2.count(8) Returns the number of items passed as argument output-> 2

L3=[7,4,8,2,12,8,34]

L3.sort() Sort items of a list in ascending order output-> [2,4,7,8,8,12,34]

L2.reverse() Reverses the list output-> L2=[8,5,8,'B','A']

L3=L2.copy() Returns a copy of the list output-> L3=['A','B',8,5,8]

List Operations

Concatenation: It concatenates the list mentioned on either side of the operator(+).

L1=[1,2,3]

L2=['Hi','X', 3]

L3=L1 + L2

Repetition: The repetition operator (*)enables the list elements to be repeated multiple times.

Iteration: The for loop is used to iterate over the list elements. for i in list1: print(i)

Membership: It returns true if a particular item exists in a particular list otherwise false.

```
In []:  list1=[1,2,3,4,5]
        for i in list1: print(i)

        1
        2
        3
        4
        5
        Buit-in Function
        len(): used to calculate the length of the list.
        max(): returns the maximum element of the list.
        min(): returns the minimum element of the list.
        sum(): Sums up the numbers in the list.
```

```
In []:  list2=[2,24,22,12,4]
        len(list2)
        max(list2)
        min(list2)
        sum(list2)
```

```
Out[ ]:    64
```

List Comprehension:

List comprehensions represent the creation of new lists from an object (like a list, set, tuple, dictionary or range) that satisfy a given condition. List comprehensions contain very compact code usually a single statement that performs the task.

```
Syntax:
newList = [expression(element) for element in old List if condition]
Eg.:
squares=[x**2 for x in range(1,11)]
```

```
In []:  squares=[x**2 for x in range(1,11)]
        print(squares)
```

```
[1, 4, 9, 16, 25, 36, 49, 64, 81, 100]
```

```
In []:  #General Form
        fruits = ["apple", "banana", "cherry", "kiwi", "mango"] newlist = []
        for x in fruits:
        if "a" in x: newlist.append(x)
        print(newlist) ['apple', 'banana', 'mango']
```

```
In []:  #List Comprehension
        fruits = ["apple", "banana", "cherry", "kiwi", "mango"] newlist = [x
        for x in fruits if "a" in x] print(newlist)
        ['apple', 'banana', 'mango']
```

Tuple in Python

Creating a Tuple The simplest way of creating a tuple is by setting a variable to a pair of empty parentheses ().

```
In []:   tuple1=()
         print(type(tuple1))
```

```
<class 'tuple'>
```
Tuple Initialization We can also specify what data exists inside it.

1. It can consist of different datatypes
2. It can also create a tuple of lists

```
In []:   tuple2=(40,50,60)
         tuple3=(45,'55','Hello World', True, 42.6)
         tuple4=([10,20],[30,40],[50,60])
```

```
In []:   tuple4[0][0]='A'
         print(tuple4)
```

```
(['A', 20], [30, 40], [50, 60])
Single Value Tuple
('A') vs ('A',)
Single value in tuple is followed by comma. i.e if we want to
initiate a tuple having value 45
then we need to write as:
my_tupple=(45,)
```

```
In []:   tuple1=(32) print(type(tuple1))
         tuple2=(12,) print(type(tuple2))
```

```
<class 'int'>
<class 'tuple'>
```

INDEXING & SLICING:

- Follow zero indexing
- Positive and Negative Indexing follows same way as a list element.
- Slicing is used to return a range of values. Like lists, tuples can also be sliced. Eg.tuple[x:y:z]

```
In []:  #positive Indexing
        tuple1 = (0, 1, 2, 3)
        print(tuple1[0]) #      Output: 0
        print(tuple1[1]) # Output: 1

        0
        1
```

```
In []:  #Negative Indexing
        tuple1 = (30, 40, 50, 60)
        print(tuple1[-1]) # Output: 60
        print(tuple1[-3]) # Output: 40

        60
        40
```

```
In []:  #Slicing (tuple[x:y:z])
        tuple1 = (1, 2, 3, 5, 8, 13)
        print(tuple1[0:3]) # Output: (1, 2, 3)
        print(tuple1[4:]) # Output: (8, 13)
        print(tuple1[0::2])

        (1, 2, 3)
        (8, 13)
        (1, 3, 8)
```

Modifying Tuples

- Tuples are immutable; i.e we couldn't change its value.

```
In []:  tuple1=(20,30,40,10)
        tuple1[2]=10000 #Python interpreter throws an error
```

```
TypeError          Traceback (most recent call last
<ipython-input-8-cc7f8eaf8b95> in <cell line: 3>()
1 tuple1=(20,30,40,10)
2
---> 3 tuple1[2]=10000 #Python interpreter throws an error
TypeError: 'tuple' object does not support item assignment
```

We can change a tuple that contains mutable objects as list etc.
For example, let us take a tuple of lists.

```
In []:  tuple1 = ([10, 20], [30, 40], [50, 60])
        tuple1[1][0] = 70
        print(tuple1)
```

```
([10, 20], [70, 40], [50, 60])
```

Tuple Methods

- len(tuple): The length method returns the length of the tuple.
- min(tuple): The min method returns the smallest element in the tuple.
- max(tuple): The max method returns the largest element in the tuple.

```
In []:  tuple1 = (10, 20, 30, 40, 50)
        print(len(tuple1))
```

```
In []:  tuple1 = (3, 9, 1, 90, 200)
        print(min(tuple1))
```

```
1
```

```
In []:  tuple1 = (3, 9, 1, 90, 200)
        print(max(tuple1))
```

```
200
```

- tuple(list): The tuple method converts the list that is passed as parameter into a tuple.
- t.count(el): The count method returns the count of the element passed as parameter.
- t.index(el): The index method returns the index of the first occurence of the element in a tuple.

```
In []:  list1 = [23, 34, 45, 56]
        lt=tuple(list1)
        print(lt)
        print(type(lt))
```

```
(23, 34, 45, 56)
<class 'tuple'>
```

```
In []:  tuple1 = (1, 24, 45, 54, 6, 34, 24)
        print(tuple1.count(24))
```

```
2
```

```
In []:  tuple1 = (1, 25, 45, 54, 45, 34, 45)
        print(tuple1.index(45))
        print(tuple1.index(45, -1)) #return the index of the last occurence
        of th
        print(tuple1.index(45, 3, 5)) #tuple specify a range to search as
        #The second paramter is the starting index, third parameter is the
        ending
```

```
2
6
4
```

Use Case: Let's assume that we have three different tuples containing the personal details of four customers. We want to create a single tuple that holds the corresponding data for each customer, including their first name, last name, and age, in the form of separate tuples

The zip() method takes multiple sequence objects and returns an iterable object by matching their elements.

```
In []:  first_names = ('Simon', 'Sarah', 'Mehdi', 'Fatime')
        last_names = ('Sinek', 'Smith', 'Lotfinejad', 'Lopes')
        ages = (49, 55, 39, 33)
```

```
zipped = zip(first_names, last_names,ages) #The zip() method takes
the th
print(zipped)
```

```
<zip object at 0x7d62c737c6c0>
```

```
In []: customers = tuple(zipped) #customers tuple consists of four tuple
                                  objec
        print(customers)
```

```
(('Simon', 'Sinek', 49), ('Sarah', 'Smith', 55), ('Mehdi',
'Lotfinejad', 39), ('Fatime', 'Lopes', 33))
```

Unpacking Tuples Unpacking a tuple allows us to extract the tuple elements and assign them to named variables.

```
In []: first_name, last_name, age = customers[0] #retrieves the tuple ele
        print(first_name,',', last_name, ',', age, 'years old')
```

```
Simon, Sinek, 49 years old
Note: List consumes more memory space compared to tuple.
```

```
In []: import sys
        a_list = ['abc', 'xyz', 123, 231, 13.31, 0.1312]
        a_tuple = ('abc', 'xyz', 123, 231, 13.31, 0.1312)
        print('The list size:', sys.getsizeof(a_list), 'bytes')
        print('The tuple size:', sys.getsizeof(a_tuple), 'bytes')
```

```
The list size: 104 bytes
The tuple size: 88 bytes
```

Dictionary in Python

```
In []: #dictionary creation #empty dictionary
        emp_dict={}
        print(type(emp_dict))
        emp_dict2=dict()
        print(type(emp_dict2))
```

```
<class 'dict'>
<class 'dict'>
```

```
In []: # dictionary with items
        demo_dict={
```

```
'key1' : 'val1',
'key2' : 'val2',
'key3' : 'val3'
}
my_dict={'name':'John', 'age':28, 'city':'New York'}
print(my_dict)
# using dict constructor
my_dict_1 = dict(name="Lisa", age=27, city="Boston")
print(my_dict_1)
```

```
{'name': 'John', 'age': 28, 'city': 'New York'}
{'name': 'Lisa', 'age': 27, 'city': 'Boston'}
```

Access Items

We can access an element by referencing its key insted of index number.

```
dictionary_name[key]
```

In []:
```
my_dict={'name': 'bob','age':34,'company': 'TATA'}
age_dict=my_dict['age']
print(age_dict)
```

```
34
```

Using Get() method

In []:
```
student={'name': 'Alex', 'age': 18, 'Class': 5, 'Country':
'USA','telephon print(student['name'])
print(student.get('telephone'))
Alex
1167
```

Add and Change items

In []:
```
my_dict={'name': 'bob','age':34,'company': 'TATA'}
#add new key
my_dict['email']='bob@abc.com'
#change the value of existing key my_dict['age']=45     #old value
is 28 print(my_dict)
```

```
{'name': 'bob', 'age': 45, 'company': 'TATA', 'email': 'bob@abc.com'}
```

Delete items

In []:
```
dict1={1:'one', 2: 'two',3:'three',4:'four','count':'number'}
#delete a key-value pair
```

```python
del dict1[3]
print(dict1)
#using pop method
print("popped value:", dict1.pop(4)) # arguement required
print("poppeditem: ", dict1.popitem()) #returns and removes the
last in
#remove all items(key-val) from dict
dict1.clear()
print(dict1)     #{} empty dictionary
#delete the entire dictionary
del dict1
print(dict1)
```

```
{1: 'one', 2: 'two', 4: 'four', 'count': 'number'} popped value: four
poppeditem: ('count', 'number')
{}
```

```
NameError                              Traceback (most recent call last
<ipython-input-6-ad033bd5807f> in <cell line: 21>()
19 #delete the entire dictionary
20 del dict1
--> 21 print(dict1)
NameError: name 'dict1' is not defined
```

Check for keys: membership

```python
In []:  my_dict = {"name":"John", "age":30, "city":"New York"}
        if "name" in my_dict: print(my_dict["name"])
        if'firstname' in my_dict: print(my_dict['firstname'])
        # use try except
        try:
        print(my_dict["firstname"])
        except KeyError: print("No key found")
```

```
John
No key found
```

Looping through dictionary

```python
In []:  loop_dict={1:'A',2:'B',3:'C',4:'D',5:'E',6:'F'}
        for key in loop_dict: print(key, loop_dict[key])
        # loop over keys
        for key in loop_dict.keys(): print(key, end = ' ')
        # loop over keys and values
```

```
print('\n')
for key, value in loop_dict.items(): print(key, value)
# loop over values
for value in loop_dict.values(): print(value, end=' ')
```

```
1    A
2    B
3    C
4    D
5    E
6    F
1 2 3 4 5 6
1    A
2    B
3    C
4    D
5    E
6    F
A B C D E F
```

fromkeys() method: takes a predefined sequence of items as an argument and returns a new dictionary with the items in the sequence set as the dictionary's specified keys.

default value is none.

dictionary_name = dict.fromkeys(sequence,value)

In []:
```
#create sequence of strings
cities = ('Paris','Athens', 'Madrid')
#create the dictionary, `my_dictionary`, using the fromkeys() method
my_dictionary = dict.fromkeys(cities)
print(my_dictionary)
#{'Paris': None, 'Athens': None, 'Madrid': None}
```

```
{'Paris': None, 'Athens': None, 'Madrid': None}
```

In []:
```
#create a sequence of strings
cities = ('Paris','Athens', 'Madrid')
#create a single value
continent = 'Europe'
my_dictionary = dict.fromkeys(cities,continent)
print(my_dictionary)
#output
```

```
#{'Paris': 'Europe', 'Athens': 'Europe', 'Madrid': 'Europe'}
```

{'Paris': 'Europe', 'Athens': 'Europe', 'Madrid': 'Europe'}

len() function returns the total length of the object that is passed as an argument.

```
In []:  my_information = {'name': 'Dionysia', 'age': 28, 'location':
        'Athens'}
        print(len(my_information))
        #output
        #3
```

3

items(): To view every key-value pair that is inside a dictionary.

```
In []:  year_of_creation = {'Python': 1993, 'JavaScript': 1995, 'HTML':
        1993}

        print(year_of_creation.items())
        #output
        #dict_items([('Python', 1993), ('JavaScript', 1995), ('HTML',
        1993)])
```

dict_items([('Python', 1993), ('JavaScript', 1995), ('HTML', 1993)])

keys() method:To see all of the keys that are inside a dictionary.

```
In []:  year_of_creation = {'Python': 1993, 'JavaScript': 1995, 'HTML':
        1993}
        print(year_of_creation.keys())
        #output

        #dict_keys(['Python', 'JavaScript', 'HTML'])
```

dict_keys(['Python', 'JavaScript', 'HTML'])

values() method:To see all of the values that are inside a dictionary,

```
In []:  year_of_creation = {'Python': 1993, 'JavaScript': 1995, 'HTML':
        1993}
        print(year_of_creation.values())
        #output
        #dict_values([1993, 1995, 1993])
```

dict_values([1993, 1995, 1993])

Merge two dictionary

Update() method

```
In []:   # existing keys are overwritten; and new keys are added
         my_dict = {'name':'Max', 'age':28, 'email':'max@xyz.com'}
         my_dict_2 = dict(name="Lisa", age=27, city="Boston")
         my_dict.update(my_dict_2)
         print(my_dict)
```

{'name': 'Lisa', 'age': 27, 'email': 'max@xyz.com', 'city': 'Boston'}

```
In []:   dict1 = {'Jessa': 70, 'Arul': 80, 'Emma': 55}
         dict2 = {'Kelly': 68, 'Harry': 50, 'Olivia': 66}
         # copy second dictionary into first dictionary
         dict1.update(dict2)
         # printing the updated dictionary
         print(dict1)
```

{'Jessa': 70, 'Arul': 80, 'Emma': 55, 'Kelly': 68, 'Harry': 50,
'Olivia': 66}

Using kwargs**

```
In []:   student_dict1 = {'Aadya': 1, 'Harry': 5, }
         student_dict2 = {'Harry': 56, 'Olivia': 6}
         student_dict3 = {'Nancy': 7, 'Perry': 9}
         # join three dictionaries
         student_dict = {**student_dict1, **student_dict2, **student_dict3}
         # printing the final Merged dictionary
         print(student_dict)
```

{'Aadya': 1, 'Harry': 56, 'Olivia': 6, 'Nancy': 7, 'Perry': 9}

Possible key types

Any immutable type, like strings or numbers, can be used as a key.

Also, a tuple can be used if it contains only immutable elements.

```
In []:   # use numbers as key, but be careful
         my_dict = {3: 9, 6: 36, 9:81}
         # do not mistake the keys as indices of a list, e.g my_dict[0] is
         not poss
         print(my_dict[3], my_dict[6], my_dict[9])
         # use a tuple with immutable elements (e.g. number, string)
         my_tuple = (8, 7) my_dict = {my_tuple: 15}
         print(my_dict) print(my_dict[my_tuple]) # print(my_dict[8, 7])
         # a list is not possible because it is not immutable # this will
         raise an Error:
```

```
my_list = [8, 7] my_dict = {my_list: 15}
```

```
9 36 81
{(8, 7): 15}
15
```

```
TypeError                              Traceback (most recent call last
<ipython-input-18-a066f4590074> in <cell line: 18>()
10 # this will raise an Error:
17 my_list = [8, 7]
--> 18 my_dict = {my_list: 15}
TypeError: unhashable type: 'list'
```

Nested Dictionaries

```
In []:  my_dict_1 = {"name": "Max", "age": 28}
        my_dict_2 = {"name": "Alex", "age": 25}
        nested_dict = {"dictA": my_dict_1,
              "dictB": my_dict_2}
        print(nested_dict)
```

```
In []:  my_dictionary = {True: "True", 1: 1, 1.1: 1.1, "one": 1,
        "languages": [" print(my_dictionary)
        #output
        #{True: 1, 1.1: 1.1, 'one': 1, 'languages': ['Python']}
```

```
In []:  my_dictionary = {["Python"]: "languages"} print(my_dictionary)
        #output
        #line 1, in <module>
        # my_dictionary = {["Python"]: "languages"}
        #TypeError: unhashable type: 'list'
```

Set in Python

Create Set

- we can use curly brackets ({ })
- or the set() constructor

```
In []:   emptySet1=set()  #set contructor
         emptySet2={}
         print(type(emptySet2))
```

```
<class 'dict'>
Initialization set
```

```
In []:   s1=set([21,12,3,'A','B',3])
         s2={1,2,3,4,1,2}
         print(type(s2))
         print(f"Set s1:{s1}")
         print(f"Set s2:{s2}")
         #s2[1]=22
```

```
<class 'set'>
Set s1:{3, 12, 21, 'B', 'A'}
Set s2:{1, 2, 3, 4}
```

```
In []:   l1=[1,2,3,34,2,4,1,'A','A']
         print(set(l1))
```

```
{1, 2, 3, 34, 4, 'A'}
```

Add and Remove Values from python Set: The method add is used to add a value to a set.

Note: only a value that is immutable (like a string or a tuple) can add to a set. For example, you would get a TypeError if you try to add a list to a set.

```
In []:   set1= set(['mango','apple','orange'])
         set1.add('papaya')
         #set1.add(['papaya','guava'])
         set1
```

```
Out []:     {'apple', 'mango', 'orange', 'papaya'}
```

```
In []:   set1.add(['grapes','guava'])
```

```
TypeError                          Traceback (most recent call last
<ipython-input-5-7948280542bb> in <cell line: 1>()
---> 1 set1.add(['grapes','guava'])
TypeError: unhashable type: 'list'
```

Remove Values from Sets in Python:

1. You can use the remove method to remove a value from a set.
2. ou can use the discard method to remove a value from a set.
3. You can also use the pop method to remove and return an arbitrary value from a set.

Remove All Values from a Python Set: You can use the clear method to remove all values from a set.

```
In []:  s1=set([1,4,9,16,25,36,49])
        s1.remove(9)
        print(s1)           #[1,4,16,25,36,49]
        #s1.remove(64)   #if you try to remove a value that is not in your
                         set, yo
        s1.discard(64)   # no key error using discard
        print(s1)
        s1.discard(49) print(s1)
        s1.pop() #pop remove and return the value
        #s2=set() #s2.pop()    #method raises a KeyError if the set is empty.
        s1.clear()
        s1
```

```
{1, 4, 36,      16,      49, 25}
{1, 4, 36,      16,      49, 25}
{1, 4, 36,      16,      25}
Out [ ]:    set()
```

Update Python Set Values:

- The update method adds the elements from a set to a set.
- It requires a single argument that can be a set, list, tuples, or dictionary.
- The. update() method automatically converts other data types into sets and adds them to the set.

```
In []:  # Initialize 3 sets
        set1 = set([7, 10, 11, 13])
        set2 = set([11, 8, 9, 12, 14, 15])
        set3 = {'d', 'f', 'h'}
        # Update set1 with set2 set1.update(set2) print(set1)
        # Update set1 with set3 set1.update(set3) print(set1)
```

```
{7, 8, 9, 10, 11, 12, 13, 14, 15}
{'h', 7, 8, 9, 10, 11, 12, 13, 14, 15, 'f', 'd'}
```

```
In []:  set_day={'Sun','Mon','Tue','Wed','Thur','Fri','Sat'} print(set_day)
        sorted(set_day)
Out [ ]:   {'Fri', 'Wed', 'Mon', 'Sun', 'Sat', 'Thur', 'Tue'}
        ['Fri', 'Mon', 'Sat', 'Sun', 'Thur', 'Tue', 'Wed']
```

As math counterparts we can perform certain operations on our sets. Union: merging two sets together.There are two ways to create a union: either with the
union() method or with the vertical bar (|) operator.

```
In []:  s1=set([2,34,12,5,7])
        s2=set([2,45,16,25,8,5])

        s_union_m=s1.union(s2)

        s_union_o=s1 | s2 print(s_union_m) print(s_union_o)
```

```
{2, 34, 5, 7, 8, 12, 45, 16, 25}
{2, 34, 5, 7, 8, 12, 45, 16, 25}
```

Intersection: To find out which names appear in both sets. The
intersection() method or the ampersand (&) operator.

```
In []:  s1=set([2,34,12,5,7])
        s2=set([2,45,16,25,8,5])
        s_intersection_m= s1.intersection(s2)
        s_intersection_o= s1 & s2
        print(s_intersection_m) print(s_intersection_o)
```

```
{2, 5}
{2, 5}
```

Difference: Difference between two sets will return all the elements that are present in the first set, but not in the second one. We can use either the difference() method or the minus sign (-)

Symmetric Difference: Result is the set of all values that are values of exactly one of two sets, but not both. We can use either the symmetric_difference() method or the sign (^)

```
In []:  s1=set([2,34,12,5,7])
        s2=set([2,45,16,25,8,5])
        s_diff_m=s1.difference(s2)
        s_diff_o= s1 - s2
        print(s_diff_m)
```

```
print(s_diff_o)
```

```
{34, 12, 7}
{34, 12, 7}
```

In []:
```
s1=set([2,34,12,5,7])
s2=set([2,45,16,25,8,5])
s_diff_m=s1.symmetric_difference(s2) s_diff_o= s1 ^ s2
print(s_diff_m) print(s_diff_o)
```

```
{16, 34, 7, 8, 25, 12, 45}
{16, 34, 7, 8, 25, 12, 45}
```

Control Flow in Python:

- Selection (Branching) Statement
- Iteration(looping)Statement
- Jumping(break/Continue) Statement

if Statement

In []:
```
age=int(input("Enter Age"))
if (age>=18):
print('You are eligible for vote')
if(age<0):
print('you entered negative number')
if(age<18):
print('Sorry….You are not eligible for vote')
```

```
Enter Age-12
you entered negative number
Sorry….You are not eligible for vote
if-else Statements
```

In []:
```
age=int(input("Enter Age"))
if (age>=18):
print('You are eligible for vote')
else:
print('you are not eligible for vote')
```

```
Enter Age-12
you are not eligible for vote
if-elif-else Statements
if-else Ladder statement(if-elif-else)
```

```
In []:   num=int(input('Enter number:'))
         if(num>0):
         print('Positive number')
         elif(num<0):
         print('Negative number')
         else:
         print('You entered Zero')
         Enter number:-12 Negative number
```

Nested if Statements

```
In []:   num=int(input('Enter number:'))
         if(num>=0): if(num>0):
         print('Positive number')
         else:
         print('You entered zero')
         else:
         print('You entered Negative number')
```

```
Enter number:45
Positive number
While Loop
```

```
In []:   count = 0
         while (count < 3):
         count = count+1 print("Hello Good Morning")
```

```
Hello Good Morning
Hello Good Morning
Hello Good Morning
```

```
In []:   num=1
         while(num<=10):
         print(num,end=" ")
         num+=1
```

```
1 2 3 4 5 6 7 8 9 10
range() Function
```

```
In []:   for i in range(5):
```

```
print(i)
```

```
0
1
2
3
4
```

In []:
```
for i in range(2,5): print(i)
```

```
2
3
4
```

In []:
```
for x in range(5,0,-1):
    print(x,end= ' ')
```

```
5 4 3 2 1
```

In []:
```
for x in range(1,10,2):
    print(x, end=' ')
```

```
1 3 5 7 9
```

In []:
```
for y in range(0,-5):
    print(y,end= ' ')
```

In []:
```
for y in range(0,-5,-1):
    print(y,end= ' ')
```

```
0 -1 -2 -3 -4
```

In []:
```
fruits=["mango","apple","grapes","cherry"]
for x in fruits: print(x)
```

```
Mango
Apple
Grapes
Cherry
Pass Statement
```

In []:
```
a=int(input("Enter first Number: "))
b=int(input("Enter Second Number: "))
if(b==0):
```

```
pass
else: print("a/b=",a/b)
```

```
Enter first Number: 24
Enter Second Number: 6
a/b= 4.0
```

In []:
```
numbers=[10,40,120,230]
for i in numbers:
if i > 100:
break
print('current number',i)
print('break is executed')
```

```
current number 10
current number 40 break is executed
Break while Loop
```

In []:
```
var='Good Morning'
size=len(var)
i=0
while(i<size):
if var[i].isspace():
break
print(var[i], end= ' ')
i=i + 1
```

```
G o o d
```

Break Nested Loop in python

In []:
```
for i in range(1, 11):
print('Multiplication table of', i)
for j in range(1, 11):
# condition to break inner loop
if i > 5 and j > 5:
break
print(i * j, end=' ')
```

```
print('')
```

```
Multiplication table of 1 1 2 3 4 5 6 7 8 9 10
Multiplication table of 2 2 4 6 8 10 12 14 16 18 20
Multiplication table of 3 3 6 9 12 15 18 21 24 27 30
Multiplication table of 4
4 8 12 16 20 24 28 32 36 40
Multiplication table of 5
5 10 15 20 25 30 35 40 45 50
Multiplication table of 6 6 12 18 24 30
Multiplication table of 7 7 14 21 28 35
Multiplication table of 8 8 16 24 32 40
Multiplication table of 9 9 18 27 36 45
Multiplication table of 10 10 20 30 40 50
```

Break Outer loop in Python:

```
In []:   for i in range(1, 11):
         # condition to break outer loop
         if i > 5:
         break
         print('Multiplication table of', i)
         for j in range(1, 11):
         print(i * j, end=' ')
         print('')
```

```
Multiplication table of 1 1 2 3 4 5 6 7 8 9 10
Multiplication table of 2 2 4 6 8 10 12 14 16 18 20
Multiplication table of 3 3 6 9 12 15 18 21 24 27 30
Multiplication table of 4
4 8 12 16 20 24 28 32 36 40
Multiplication table of 5
5 10 15 20 25 30 35 40 45 50
Continue Statement in for loop
```

```
In []:   num= [3,7,11,18]
         for i in num:
         print('current value is: ', i)
         if i > 10:
         continue
         square =i * i
```

```python
print('square of a current number is', square)
```

```
current value is: 3
square of a current number is 9 current value is: 7
square of a current number is 49 current value is: 11
current value is: 18
In while loop
```

In []:
```python
new_var = 8
while new_var >0:
new_var=new_var-1
if new_var==2:
continue
print(new_var)
print("loop end")
```

```
7
6
5
4
3
1
0
loop end
Continue Statement in Nested Loop
```

In []:
```python
for i in range(1,6):
print('Multiplication table of', i)
for j in range(1, 11):
# condition to skip current iteration
if j == 3:
continue
print(i * j, end=' ')
print('')
```

```
Multiplication table of 1
1 2 4 5 6 7 8 9 10
Multiplication table of  2
2 4 8 10 12 14 16 18 20
Multiplication table of
3 3 6 12 15 18 21 24 27 30
Multiplication table of 4 4 8 16 20 24 28 32 36 40
Multiplication table of 5 5 10 20 25 30 35 40 45 50
```

Continue Statement in Outer loop

```
In []:   for i in range(1, 6):
         # condition to skip iteration
         # Don't print multiplication table of even numbers
         if i% 2 == 0:
         continue
         print('Multiplication table of', i)
         for j in range(1, 11):
         print(i * j, end=' ')
         print('')
```

```
Multiplication table of 1
1 2 3 4 5 6 7 8 9 10
Multiplication table of  3
3 6 9 12 15 18 21 24 27  30
Multiplication table of 5
5 10 15 20 25 30 35 40 45 50
```

FUNCTIONS IN PYTHON

Built-in function

```
In []: print('hello,students')
       print(15)
       #Is print return a value???????
```

```
hello,students
15
```

```
In []: mylength=len('Welcome Class')
       print(mylength)
```

```
14
```
User-define Function

```
In []: def write():                    #function name is message having no pa
       print('Welcome to python class')              # function body
       write()
       print(write())   #function calling
```

```
Welcome to python class
Welcome to python class
None
```
Function with parameters and arguments

```
In []: def message(name): #function message have a variable as a parameter
       print('Hi', name)
       message('John')    # the actual value is ('James') passed as an argum
```

```
Hi John
```

```
In []: #output of the code???
       def read(name):
       print('Hi ' + name)
       print("Let's greet the entire world")
```

```
read('world')
```

Let's greet the entire world
Hi world
Returning values

```
In []: def add(a, b):
       return a + b      #keyword return used to return a value from our func
       result = add(4, 9)
       print('The addition of given two number is: ', result)
```

The addition of given two number is: 13
Empty Return Statement

```
In []: def select(name):
       if name.startswith('X'):
       # We don't select people with weird names: p
       return 0
       print('Hi there, ', name)
       print(select('AlXander'))
```

Hi there, AlXander
None

```
In []: def stmnt(a,b):
       c= a+b
       return c
       result=stmnt(1,5)
       print(result)
```

6

```
In []: #Find the even numbers from given list of numbers
       def is_even(list1):
       even_num = []
       for n in list1:
       if n% 2 == 0:
       even_num.append(n)
       # return a list
       return even_num
       # Pass list to the function
       even_num = is_even([2, 3, 42, 51, 62, 70, 5, 9])
       print("Even numbers are:", even_num)
```

Even numbers are: [2, 42, 62, 70]

```
In []:  #Return multiple values
        def arithmetic(num1, num2): add = num1 + num2
        sub = num1 - num2
        multiply = num1 * num2
        division = num1 / num2 # return four values
        return add, sub, multiply, division
        # read four return values in four variables
        a, b, c, d = arithmetic(10, 2)
        print("Addition: ", a)
        print("Subtraction: ", b)
        print("Multiplication: ", c)
          print("Division: ", d)
```

```
Addition: 12
Subtraction: 8
Multiplication: 20
Division: 5.0
Scope of Variable
```

```
In []:  #local scope
        def f():
        num=12
        return num
        #print('the number is:', num) #error 'num is not defined' due to
        local sc
        print('the number is: ', f())
```

```
the number is: 12
```

```
In []:  #global scope
        num=12
        def f():
        print('inside function', num)
        return num
        print('outside function', num)
        f()
```

```
outside function 12
inside function 12
12
```

```
Out[]:
```

```
In []: num=12
       def f():
       global num
       num+=2
       print('inside function', num)
       return num
       print('outside function', num)
       f()
```

```
Out[]:
```

```
In []: global_test = 'DataScience'
       def var_scope():
       local_test = 'Python'
       print(local_test)
       var_scope()
       # Output 'Python'
       # outside of function
       print(global_test)
       # Output 'DataScience'
       # NameError: name 'local_test' is not defined #print(local_test)
```

```
outside function 12
inside function 14
14
Python
DataScience
```

Local Variable in function:

- Declared inside the function
- Not accessible from outside of the function

```
In []: #Local Variable
       def function1():
       # local variable
       loc_var = 888
       print("Value is: ", loc_var)
       def function2():
       pass
       #print("Value is: ", loc_var)
       function1() function2()
```

```
Value is: 888
```

Global Variable:

- Declared outside of the function
- Scope of a global variable is broad.
- Accessible in all functions of the same module.

```
In []:   #Global Variable in function
         global_var = 999
         def function1():
             print("Value in 1nd function: ", global_var)
         def function2():
             print("Value in 2nd function: ", global_var)
         function1()
         function2()
```

```
Value in 1nd function: 999
Value in 2nd function: 999
```

What if we want to change the value of global variable inside a function?
The way to change the value of a global variable inside a function is by using
the global keyword

```
In []:   x=20     #global variable
         def my_fun():
         global x
         x = x+30          # modify global variable x
         print('global variable x inside a function:', x)
         print('global variable x outside a function:', x)
         #before calling a func


         my_fun()
         print('global variable x outside a function:', x)
         #after calling a funct
```

```
global variable x outside a function: 20
global variable x inside a function: 50
global variable x outside a function: 50
```

Global Keyword in function

'global' is the keyword used to access the actual global variable from outside
the function. we use the global keyword for two purposes:

- To declare a global variable inside the function.

- Declaring a variable as global, which makes it available to function to perform the modification.

```
In []:   # Global variable
         global_var = 5
         def function1():
         print("Value in 1st function: ", global_var)
         def function2():
         # Modify global variable
         # function will treat it as a local variable
         global_var = 555
         print("Value in 2nd function: ", global_var)
         def function3():
         print("Value in 3rd function: ", global_var)
         function1()
         function2()
         function3()
```

```
Value in 1st function: 5
Value in 2nd function: 555
Value in 3rd function: 5
```

```
In []:   #global scope
         ii = 50 #defined in the global scope
         def fan():
         ii = 100#defined in local scope
         return ii
         result=fan()    #The local scope is used when there is a collision
                         with a v #of the same name in the global scope.
         print(ii)
         print('The value stored from function is: ', result)
```

```
50
The value stored from function is: 100
```

```
In []:   ii=50
         def fan():
         global ii
         ii = 100
         return ii
         res=fan()
         print(ii)
         print(res)
```

```
100
100
```

Nested Function: Function in Function:

- It's a concept of a "nested function" or "inner function", which is simply a function defined inside another function.
- Outer function has to be called in order for the inner function to execute. If the outer function is not called, the inner function will never execute.
- A nested function can access the variables defined in the function in which it is create.

```
In []:  def outer():      # outer function
        print("This is outer function")
        def inner():
        print("This is inner function")
        inner() # calling inner function
        outer() # calling outer function
```

```
This is outer function
This is inner function
```

```
In []:  #Outer function has to be called in order for the inner function to
        execut
        def function1():        # outer function
        print ("Hello from outer function")
        def function2():        # inner function
        print ("Hello from inner function")
```

```
function2()
```

```
In []:  # Inner function can access the variable x defined in its parent
        function
        def outer(): # outer function
        x = 10
        def inner():
        print("Inside inner func", x)
        inner() # calling inner function
        print("Inside outer func", x)
        outer() # calling outer function
```

```
Inside inner func 10
Inside outer func 10
```

```
In []:  def outer_fun(a, b):
        def inner_fun(c, d):
        return c + d
```

```python
    return inner_fun(a, b)
res = outer_fun(5, 10)
print(res)
```

15

```python
In []:  # without Nested Function
        import math
        def circle_area(rad1,rad2):
        area1= math.pi*rad1**2
        area2=math.pi*rad2**2
        return area1,area2
        circle_area(12.5,15)
```

Out[]: (490.8738521234052, 706.8583470577034)

```python
In []:  # using Nested Function
        def circle_area(rad1,rad2):
        def area_calculate(radius):
        area= math.pi*radius**2
        return area
        return(area_calculate(rad1),area_calculate(rad2))
        a1,a2= circle_area(12.5,15)
        print(a1,a2)
```

490.8738521234052 706.8583470577034

```python
In []:  #Value of outer function variable is not change inside the inner
        function.
        def function1():          # outer function
        x = 2                # A variable defined withi
        def function2(a):        # inner function
        # Let's define a new variable within the inner function
        x = 6
        print (a+x)
        print (x)                 # to display the value of x
        function2(3)
        function1()
```

2

9

```python
In []:  # Nested Function provide us encapsulation
        def outer_function(x):
        # Hidden from the outer code
```

```
def inner_increment(x):
return x + 2
y = inner_increment(x)
print(x, y)
#inner_increment(5)
outer_function(5)
```

5 7

In []:
```
# Local Variable can't accesible outside the body
def chair():
price = 99
return price
print(price)                #Name define Error for price
```

```
NameError                      Traceback (most recent call last
<ipython-input-3-859515da3008> in <cell line: 6>()
4   return price
5
—> 6 print(price)        #Name define Error for price
NameError: name 'price' is not defined
```

In []:
```
ii = 50 #global variable
def fan():
ii = 100# local variable
return ii
result=fan()     # local ii value
print(ii)        # global ii value
print('The value stored from function is: ', result)
```

50
The value stored from function is: 100

In []:
```
def add_num(c,d):
return c+d
return c
add_num(5,7)
```

Out[]: 12

```
In []:   def add(a, b):
         return a+5, b+5
         result = add(3, 2)
         print(result)
         (8, 7)
```

Python Function Arguments

Positional Arguments: In positional arguments, arguments are stuck to a specific order to pass in function calling according to defining the function.

```
def employee_data (name, age):
    print (f'Employee name is {name}. I am {age} years old.')
employee_data ('John', 45)      # positional arguments are in function
                                  calling
employee_data (45, 'john')      # This is doesn't


    Employee name is John. I am 45 years old.
    Employee name is 45. I am john years old.
```

Keyword Arguments: Keyword arguments are labeled with keywords with the values passed in function calling.

```
employee_data(age=45,name='John')


    Employee name is John. I am 45 years old.


def fruits(a, b, p):
    print('We have', a+ ',', b+ ' and', p+ ' at our store.')
#fruits('apple', 'banana', 'pineapple')
fruits('apple', b = 'banana', p = 'pineapple')
fruits(b='banana', p='pineapple', 'apple')      # Show the error



# Note: The keyword arguments must always come after the positional
arguments.
employee_data('James',age= 45)
#employee_data(name='jojo', 56)


    Employee name is James. I am 45 years old.
```

Default Arguments: In default arguments, we can set the default value to the arguments that are used for any missing arguments.

```python
def greet(name, message='Hello'):
    print(f'{message}, {name}!')
greet ('Allen')
greet ('John', 'Hey')
```

```
    Hello, Allen!
    Hey, John!
```

```python
# non-default arguments can not be followed by default arguments we have
default values for all the arguments to their right def num(b,c,a=10):
print('the values are:')
print(a)
print(b)
print(c)
num(14,5)
```

```
    the values are:
    10
    14
    5
```

```python
def class_detail(name, subject='maths'):
print(f'The student name is: {name} and subject is {subject}')

class_detail('Shree')
class_detail('allen')
class_detail('Ram','English')
```

```
The student name is: Shree and subject is maths
The student name is: allen and subject is maths
The student name is: Ram and subject is English
```

Arbitrary Arguments: This type of argument is used when the number of arguments is not known by the programmer and represented by asterisk(*)

```python
def class_student(*name):
    print('registered Student list')
    for i in name:
```

```
        print(i)
  class_student('Ash', 'Riya', 'James', 'Jojo')
```

```
registered Student list
Ash
Riya
James
Jojo
```

Lambda Function

It is an anonymous function created using *lambda* keyword.

```
lambda x, y: x+y
_(1,2) # expression evaluated using underscore(_)
```

```
3
```

```
(lambda x: x + 1)(2)
```

```
3
```

```
# if-else using lambda function
print((lambda x: x if(x > 10) else 10)(5))
```

```
10
```

```
# multiple conditions are present(if-elif-…-else)
(lambda x: x * 10 if x > 10 else (x * 5 if x < 5 else x))(11)
```

```
110
```

www.ingramcontent.com/pod-product-compliance
Lightning Source LLC
Chambersburg PA
CBHW031129130726
47988CB00006B/2290